ENTREPRENEUR'S
FIELD
MANUAL

ENTREPRENEUR'S
FIELD
MANUAL

Lessons learned bootstrapping one of
the fastest growing businesses in America

ERNIE BRAY

Entrepreneur's Field Manual: Lessons learned bootstrapping one of the fastest growing businesses in America

ISBN-13: 978-0-9842036-7-3

Cover design: Mike Stecker
Interior design: Adina Cucicov

Disclaimer

This book contains business strategies, marketing methods and other business advice that, regardless of my own results and experience, may not produce the same results (or any results) for you.

We make absolutely no guarantee, expressed or implied, that by following the advice or content available from this book you will make any money or attain any success, as there are many factors and variables that come into play regarding any given business. The reality is most businesses fail.

The information provided within this book is for general informational purposes only. While we try to keep the information up-to-date and correct, there are no representations or warranties, express or implied, about the completeness, accuracy, reliability, suitability or availability with respect to the information, products, services, or related graphics contained in this book for any purpose. Any use of this information is at your own risk.

I dedicate this book to my wife, who has supported me in everything I do.

And to my dad, mom, and brother for helping build the foundation of who I am today, and to my boys Ben and Hunter and nephew Sawyer. I hope this inspires all of you to go out and achieve your dreams!

CONTENTS

PREFACE

TOSS around the word entrepreneur these days, and people get excited. It's a status symbol with so many young people clamoring to be the next Zuckerberg or Musk. Young kids want to be YouTubers, run their own gaming companies, and become the next Instagram star. In fact, for many, this appeals even more than becoming an athlete, actor, or musician. These days, a famous YouTuber can even outshine other celebrities in popularity. The lure of making it big, getting massive publicity, having huge houses and a fleet of fancy cars has led to a glamorization of "entrepreneurship." Is it good or bad? Well, as inspiration for those to go out and achieve, it might be great but what many people don't realize is that true entrepreneurship is hard work and much different than the fake images you see on the internet. It can be a great journey, but you have to really put in the effort! While the news and media publicize the outliers who reach mega success, most entrepreneurs toil endless hours to build a successful business outside of the limelight. This is where the real success stories are.

With all of the technology and avenues to create content that never existed in the past, opportunities have opened up at a level unseen before. Becoming an entrepreneur is now the "dream" for so many, but the entrepreneurial spirit is not new. In fact, it is deeply woven into our national psyche. Early in our history, launching a business was often born of necessity. As immigrants arrived on these shores and pioneers headed west, both seeking economic opportunity, they established farms and opened feed stores, mills, tack shops, and other small businesses—providing goods and services to other citizens.

Today, though people launch companies for many different reasons, all entrepreneurs share certain traits—including a desire to take charge of their lives, a passion for succeeding, and the ability to persevere in the face of intimidating odds. And even if you're successful, you can never rest on your laurels. You must continuously push forward, or the competition will overtake you—probably sooner than you think.

Before founding Auto Claims Direct (ACD), I spent years as a "cubicle jockey" in the insurance industry, working jobs I didn't always like and where I wasn't always appreciated. During this time, however, I kept my eyes and my mind open. I was keen to learn new things, aware that I didn't know everything—and in some cases, didn't even know how much I didn't know. Thanks to this open-mindedness, I soon realized that the insurance industry had a need for something new. That "something new" was a unified, high-tech, auto claims platform that would connect service providers with each other and with their customers—a platform that would provide higher visibility to everyone at an insurance company. In other words, I spotted a "value vacancy," an opportunity to exploit an untapped niche in the market.

I'm good at saving and managing money, so when the time came, my wife and I sold our home and used our savings and proceeds to launch ACD. I had to balance our investment, live on a tight budget, and do the work to build a business! In this respect, I was a fairly typical entrepreneur: A 2006 Wells Fargo/Gallup Small Business Index Study found that 73 percent of small business owners rely primarily on savings to finance their startups, while 37 percent use small business loans or lines of credit.

Of course, capitalizing the venture was hardly the only hurdle I had to overcome. The biggest challenge was overcoming obscurity in a crowded market—and trust—among prospective clients to land our first few contracts. Because ACD was entering a highly competitive industry, we struggled to create a reputable brand and to land clients—clients who already had a wealth of established firms from which to choose. Although I believed ACD could provide services and technology that were far superior to the "old guard," convincing prospects wasn't easy. As an unknown face in the crowd, we were at a disadvantage. Why should insurance companies (or any company) trust us to get the job done?

We had to build credibility, and we had to build a track record. Both tasks required patience and perseverance.

We started small, with only four people—but over 15 years, we grew to 40. Some people may consider that fast growth; some may consider it slow. To me, it doesn't matter. We've grown because we succeeded in establishing a reputation as a top-notch provider of auto claims services and technology.

Since 2003, ACD has earned numerous national awards, including seven rankings on *Inc. Magazine*'s "America's fastest-growing private companies" list and four years on Deloitte's "North America Technology Fast 500™" rankings.

I've decided to open up my playbook to reveal and explain some of the strategies and tactics I've used to build a successful 8-figure company. So whether you're thinking of taking the entrepreneurial leap or merely seeking a few insights to help your established company, this book is for you. My mission is to give you some no-nonsense nuggets of advice and raw, straight-to-the-point tips from my personal experience. When you put your savings and your reputation on the line, you quickly notice what works and what doesn't.

I hope this book helps fuel your drive and inspires you to amazing achievements!

WHO WANTS TO BE AN ENTREPRENEUR?

Some time ago, I conducted a survey of 500 random people, and I found that 17 percent either owned or were currently starting a business. That left 83 percent who were employees. Of those employees, however, 63 percent either wanted to—or would consider—becoming an entrepreneur. Of course, many of these people are afraid to strike out on their own because they fear failure and financial insecurity. That's understandable, but in today's economic climate, there's no such thing as a guaranteed job or career. Too often, financial security is merely an illusion.

I never dreamed of becoming an entrepreneur before I received a dose of real world reality. I bought into the idea that a college degree would instantly open doors to a high-paying job, but after graduating from college, I quickly found myself in a cubicle doing inside sales for an electrical supply company. That entry-level slap-in-the-face job was the catalyst that spurred me to greater heights. From that time forward, I had a burning desire to become a business leader.

Moving from a cubicle to running your own show is your decision. Trying to advance your career by simply showing up to work won't cut it. You must take control. You must seize opportunities!

Do you believe you can offer more, but don't know where to start? Then test the waters before taking the ultimate plunge. You might discover that owning a part-time business satisfies your goal. Or you might realize that you want more. Conduct research, check out different business models, search for value vacancies, and take "baby steps" toward launching a business until you figure out what will work and, most important, what truly inspires you.

YOU WANT A HOBBY OR A BUSINESS?

I was recently asked, "How do you maintain so much drive and energy for your business?" The answer: I thrive on the excitement of building relationships, planning strategy, igniting the spirit of competition, brainstorming ideas, and making a positive difference in people's lives.

It's important to note, however, that simply enjoying your business versus feeling *driven* by the business is often the difference between pursuing a hobby and creating a lucrative enterprise. Many people have ideas for *avocations* that they'd love to monetize. They might want to make and sell pottery, form a rock band, flip a house, or write a book. Although they may view any of these pursuits as a "side business"—a way to generate extra income—such businesses rarely evolve beyond hobbies.

For example, my wife and I once enjoyed building custom wooden benches and tables. It was fun, and we toyed with the idea of turning these hobbies into a business. But eventually, we realized that we'd have to invest all our energy and time in these pursuits to have any chance of succeeding.

A hobby is relaxing; something you enjoy. If you make a little money, great. If you don't, that's also fine. However, unless you're willing to pour most of your time and resources into the avocation, it will never become a genuine business. It won't become a genuine business until you move beyond "fun" to "very serious"—from *"it would be nice to earn some money"* to *"this company is our primary source of income."*

Business can be fun, but a business differs from a hobby in that fun is not its *raison d'être*. Serving others (consumers, employees, and entire communities) and generating profits are the main reasons for launching a business—in that order.

Chapter One

MENTAL PREPARATION

TAKE CONTROL OF YOUR DESTINY

As I mentioned in the Intro, I was once a cubicle jockey, trapped in a three-walled cell. If this describes your situation, I have an important piece of advice: Don't resign yourself to this fate. You *can* control your destiny.

While sitting in that cubicle, I knew I had to do something. I wasn't sure what the "something" was, but I knew I'd never be happy in a 90-square-foot prison. I wanted to get out there and achieve a dream. It was obvious that nobody else would advance my career. In fact, nobody at the company even cared if I had a good idea. It was up to me to blaze a career path that would unleash my ideas and talents.

If you want to be heard at your company, speak up. But if you have a burning entrepreneurial drive, strike out on your own. Take purposeful steps to advance your dream of owning a business. Before you start, however, you should mentally prepare for some risk-taking. Your mindset should be "I'm going to do something *more* than commute to work, punch the clock, check out at five o'clock, and go home to watch TV." Instead, you must set aside enough time—30 to 60 minutes on weeknights, and at least three to four hours on weekends—to advance your dream. The difference between an entrepreneur and a "wantrepreneur" is that the latter gets mired in the dreaming stage and never takes *action*.

What steps should you take?

First, research the industry you want to enter. Second, start building the infrastructure you'll need to launch the business. Third, get out there and do it. Dip your toes in the waters and test them. Test the waters by investing enough time and mental energy to determine whether your ideas, and your business model, are viable.

DON'T EXPECT IT TO BE EASY

One thing is certain in business: there will always be roadblocks. You'll never a reach a point where everything works exactly as planned. Even if you achieve this "commercial nirvana," it will be short-lived. Someone or something will eventually toss a wrench into your paradise. And that's fine. It's normal. You can't let setbacks cause you sleepless nights and (too much) stress. Things worth achieving are never easy. The sooner you realize this, the better you'll focus on developing solutions to the problems.

Unfortunately, we live in a culture rife with get-rich-quick schemes and schemers—con artists who lead millions of Americans to believe that *everyone else* has become an instant billionaire while they've been obsessing over the latest celebrity. Among other things, these schemers give people the impression that running a business is easy—that all it takes to succeed is attending a one-hour webinar and then creating a website to sell online products while sitting at the beach. Needless to say, these dreams of overnight riches rarely pan out (except for the scammers who peddle the dreams).

Launching a sustainable business is anything but easy. That's why so few people try and even fewer succeed. Most people are in love with the *idea* of running a business, but quickly abandon the dream when they see how much work and frustration is involved. They return to their cubicles and former recreational activities the moment they realize that the initial return on investment is not buckets of cash, but still *more* work and frustration.

Few people have the perseverance to play the "long game." Those who *do* persevere, know that once they launch the business, there's no turning back. They have to keep pushing forward; they have to keep setting goals; and they will probably have to settle for small victories—at least in the beginning.

Even if your goals change over time, your passion and zest for a life of positive accomplishment is something worth striving for. You might start the venture with one goal in mind, but then discover a new ambition midstream—one that leads to completely different achievements. Always remember: What many people consider "failure" is actually vital feedback.

Starting a business is exciting. But once that first flush of enthusiasm fades, entrepreneurs have to summon some serious slow-burning motivation to continue doing the dirty work. Building a business takes years of slog and inner drive. If you have an enthusiastic personality, self-belief, competitiveness, commitment, and a desire for perfection, then you have the winning formula. If you don't, you need to cultivate these attributes. Are you able to forgo your favorite Sunday football games? Are you willing to work nights instead of staring at your iPhone? If so, you have far more drive and commitment than any "wantrepreneur" will ever have.

ALWAYS DO WHAT IS RIGHT

At some point, every entrepreneur will be tempted to take shortcuts rather than doing the right thing. You will inevitably encounter ways to move your business forward that are either dishonest or deceitful. Although maintaining high standards is easier said than done for some people, it's critical to maintain your honor and integrity—to follow a personal code that doesn't permit the slightest impropriety.

At ACD, for example, I've encountered situations like this: A claims adjuster at an insurance company is promoted to a management position. Before he takes over the job, he calls to say, "Now that I'm going to be the claims manager, how are you going to show me some love?" In other words, *what are you going to do for me*?

I've heard rumors that some vendors offer kickbacks to get the business in a situation like this. Regardless of whether these rumors are true, we don't play that way. It's tempting to rationalize this sort of behavior by saying, "What's wrong with a little 'gift' to ensure that we win new business? After all, the additional revenue will benefit not just me, but also my employees and their families." The problem is, once you rationalize unethical behavior on a small scale, it becomes easier to excuse behavior that's even worse, including illegal conduct.

In addition to becoming the kind of organization that will do anything for a buck, you may well shift your company's focus from creating innovative products, services, and strategies to a focus on developing a playbook of dirty tricks and underhanded schemes. Rather than becoming a thought leader, you'll become (and be known as) a dishonest manipulator.

History shows us that corrupt leaders and companies rarely thrive over the long haul. At some point, unethical and illegal practices are exposed, and unpleasant consequences ensue.

The bottom line: Run an ethical and professional company because it's the right thing to do. Your firm may not grow as fast as you want, at least not initially. Sure, your competitors may steal some seemingly valuable business from you. But ultimately, your reputation is your most important asset, one that's much more valuable than short-term profits.

SYNCHRONIZE YOUR WATCH TO LOMBARDI TIME

Vince Lombardi was one of the greatest National Football League coaches in history, preaching hard work and dedication. The basic premise of "Lombardi Time" is *promptness*. Always show up for a designated meeting 15 minutes before the scheduled time. Arriving early ensures that you won't be late, demonstrates commitment, and allows you to do last-minute prep work. The individual who arrives early demonstrates concern for others' time, especially when compared with someone who's perpetually late, which is a hallmark of unreliability.

If you're late for a presentation to a prospect or a key client, you *will* make a bad impression. Although people may seemingly let you off the hook, pretending that it's "no big deal," they *will* remember the transgression and hold it against you, regardless of why you arrived late (heavy traffic, flight delays, etc.). Tardiness demonstrates poor planning. People who are always on time have enough respect for others' time to make sure they are *never* late—even if this causes some inconvenience. For example, I once knew a business owner who always took a flight the night before an important meeting—just in case he encountered a flight delay or other inconvenience.

Arriving early can spell the difference between landing or losing a new account.

CONFIDENCE IS A MUST

According to an article in the *Journal of Finance,* a 10-year study demonstrates that overconfident CEOs are better leaders. When you think about it, this makes sense: Extreme confidence empowers people to make quick decisions, while those who lack confidence are usually more tentative. Of course, there's a delicate balance between audaciousness and arrogance, so this attribute requires careful cultivation.

To lead a successful business, you need to have faith in yourself—faith that your ideas, visions, and actions are the best. It's wise to consider input from trusted advisors, but when it's time to decide, you must move forward with confidence. Make decisions with an assurance that motivates and inspires your whole team. In this age of consensus and groupthink, the importance of decisive leadership cannot be overstated.

People sometimes say that I "shoot from the hip." It's true. I *do* make quick decisions. I believe that listening to your instincts and tackling problems immediately is better than waffling. If you see a problem with your staff, address it right away by telling the employees how to fix it.

For example, if I notice that a new call-center employee is mishandling a customer call, I take instant action. Instead of letting the worker complete the call—and possibly botch it—I intervene. Initially, I signal the employee to determine and let me know whether he needs help, but if necessary, I'll take over the call and resolve the situation to the customer's satisfaction. Afterward, I make sure the employee receives additional training so he can do a better job in the future. The reason is that every opportunity, every experience with a customer, can be a make-or-break situation. So if you see a situation going south, address it ASAP.

Case in point: We once had an employee who appeared to be handling accounts well in documenting files, but his tone on the phone was somewhat rough with clients. After the other team members brought this to my attention, I stood back, listened, and noticed that the employee was trying, but he lacked some of the finer points of empathy with customers. Though he was delivering the correct message, the tone and method needed work. I discussed this with him and provided needed training, and the employee improved. The point here is that as a leader, you have to take action.

Allowing problems to fester can cause things to spiral out of control, promoting bad work habits within the entire organization. My advice: Trust your instincts and make fast (but informed) decisions. You'll sometimes face complex situations that require time for contemplation and deliberation, but don't waste time overthinking *everything*.

NEVER GO OUT ON A MISS

This comes from my basketball days. Never end your day with a failure. This is a lesson learned from my years of playing competitive basketball. When practicing, I never left for the day unless I made my last shot. If I missed, I would mentally be allowing myself to leave with a failure. Even though it might not seem to matter to other people, in my mind, small wins and losses add up over time and create patterns. It's better to leave the basketball court after chalking up a "win." This generates a lingering feeling of accomplishment.

If you're having a bad day, don't leave the office until you achieve something positive, no matter how small it may be. It's imperative to always go out on top. Work on a project that will help move your company forward. Try to regain some forward momentum that will give you a mental boost for the next morning. Focusing on what went wrong is just counter-productive.

Chapter Two

CREATE THE CONCEPT

DEVELOP SOMETHING OF VALUE

What's the first step in launching a viable enterprise?

Creating a product, service, or niche solution that nobody else can match.

At ACD, we created a valuable service line by learning our customers' pain-points and brainstorming solutions for them. As part of the process, we asked customers lots of questions, and we actively listened to their responses. If we heard someone say, "I wish we had *this* solution to *that* problem," we debated ways to transform that wish into a reality. By doing this, we sometimes discovered niches we hadn't known about. But we usually had to *ask* these customers and prospects, because most people aren't in the habit of complaining to strangers about their problems and challenges.

We also took care to query a large enough cross-section of customers and potential customers before moving forward with a new product or service. It's important that you confirm a consistent theme or pattern in the target market. Only then, can you be certain that you've uncovered an actual niche rather than a smattering of "outlier complaints."

Don't overthink things. The vast majority of marketable inventions and innovations are just incremental improvements to existing products, services, and technologies—they're not game-changing blockbusters. In other words, don't insist on reinventing the wheel. Instead, start by considering a new twist to an existing product or service. By doing this, you'll probably find plenty of opportunities to carve a unique position in the marketplace. You don't have to invent the next social media craze or become the hottest new tech firm, to be wildly successful. More often, it's the simplest ideas in the "boring" industries that prove the most profitable.

Look around. Could a small, but fresh, new idea change the landscape? How? Keep your mind open. Think of ways to enhance an existing process or product.

Of course, developing an offering that's superior to your competitors' is one thing; persuading prospects to buy it is something else. To be successful, you must first provide value, and then effectively communicate that value with promotional claims that can be proven.

A customer today does not necessarily mean a customer tomorrow, so you'll need to provide ongoing value, innovation, and amazing service to stay relevant. Find ways to add desirable new products and services to your menu—offerings that will keep your company at the top of your clients' minds. Although it's essential to specialize in at least one core product or service, it's also a good idea to periodically introduce something fresh to ensure that the core solution is up-to-date and distinct from competitors'. But don't stray too far from the core offerings of your mission. Don't diversify into new areas just for the sake of being different or because your rivals have done so. There's always a risk that you could dilute your brand or, if you wander too far from your capabilities, become known as a second-rate provider.

FAILURE CAN PROVIDE VALUABLE FEEDBACK

Before launching ACD, I pursued several other ventures. I enjoyed some small successes, but each business eventually fizzled, thanks to a lack of focus. I co-founded an online country music magazine and a fitness-coaching site, and I sold real estate. I had high hopes for each company. What I didn't have was enough passion and commitment.

I don't view these attempts as failures, though, but as worthwhile experiences. I still draw on the lessons learned by running each of them. This supports my belief that sometimes one must fail in order to succeed. The simple reality is that your next big attempt to develop a new product or service may not "succeed," but nevertheless, could produce an amazing outcome.

On one occasion, I decided that ACD would develop a new technology platform for a particular niche in the insurance industry. After giving my team all the information and specs needed to create the product, I made the mistake of ceding full control of the project to the tech team. Without ongoing guidance from management, they built a solution that worked, but one that was clunky and didn't satisfy clients' needs. After sifting through customer feedback, what we learned—beyond the fact that clients didn't like the platform—was that the tech team lacked proper procedures for constructing a winning solution. The product development process contained no checks and balances.

More specifically, we learned that, before building any new products, we first needed to create a standardized, multi-staged, development plan. Among other things, we needed a design phase to allow for give-and-take between the tech team and the rest of the staff; we needed a stage to internally test ideas and prototypes; and we needed a beta-testing period with select clients.

In the end, we transformed failure into a new and better product development process. So in a very real way, that failure paved the way for our success. All development since has been done using this new process. Thanks to this mini-disaster, we received invaluable feedback that prompted us to design a model that produces solutions better, faster, and cheaper.

FOCUS ON MORE THAN MONEY

Obviously, your company needs to earn money. Eventually. In my experience, however, it's a mistake to focus *solely* on money. In fact, the more you focus on money, the worse you'll do. Instead, concentrate on delivering unbeatable services and products. If you succeed at doing this, the money will follow.

Business leaders must be fiercely committed to their ideas, products, or services—or all three. If your primary focus is on bringing in money *today*, you can expect to face some insurmountable struggles. Focus on creating a smooth-running company that offers valuable solutions. This will foster customer excitement, which will encourage customer loyalty, which will lead to financial gains.

After experiencing a taste of success, too many entrepreneurs become obsessed with the trappings of executive status—expensive cars, vacations, and second homes. When you succumb to this, your attention wanders from your core purpose, which is providing customers with valuable solutions. There are plenty of ways to make a lot of money if that's all you want to do. Running a business has never been a fast and easy way to make bucket-loads of cash.

I know it seems counterintuitive, but your focus should not be on profits, but on improving your wares and customer relationships. The more you focus on the latter, the more you'll enhance your company's reputation—and attract new customers.

There are many ways to fail: poor marketing, an incompetent sales force, being late to market. But the #1 way to run a company into the ground is failing to develop compelling, high-quality products or services. You can obsess over profits as much as you like, but if you don't pay attention to the fundamentals, your venture doesn't stand a chance.

READ, TALK, LEARN, & GROW YOUR KNOWLEDGE

I gain both inspiration and knowledge from reading about successful companies and their leaders. If I acquire just one tidbit of information that I can apply to my company, I consider the book-reading effort well spent. My advice is to read as much as possible and soak up that information like a sponge. It's energizing to learn how others have become successful by analyzing their methods. I especially enjoy books that offer strategic advice and stories about entrepreneurs who overcame huge challenges. They provide useful tips, motivational case histories, and plenty of ideas to explore.

One of the most invigorating aspects of starting a business is dreaming big and setting goals. If you've been thinking of launching a company, you've probably discussed your ideas with friends and family. That's great. That's essential. It usually takes a series of conversations to fully develop plans in your own mind. You can receive valuable input. Some may disagree with me, but merely talking about your ideas with others can be the catalyst you need to actually get started. My wife and I still go to a restaurant to brainstorm now and then—it's a great way to develop new ideas. The key, though, is you have to take action after you talk!

Chapter Three

EQUIP YOURSELF

MODEL SUCCESS

Observing and analyzing the paths and traits of respected business leaders allows you to borrow some of their genius. Just remember, everyone has faults, so focus on the gathering the best and creating your own unique formula.

For example, I've long been a fan of Apple and Steve Jobs. I've also read books about former General Electric CEO Jack Welch, as well as the innovators behind Trader Joe's and many others... so I don't emulate just one leader or company or business model. Instead, I try to find the best ideas, the ideas that make the most sense, from wherever I can, and then apply those ideas to my own situation. Before launching my company, I focused mostly on business models that would help me create *a company that was respected for its quality, innovation, and customer service*—and for being a great place to work.

I believe in studying as many successful people as I can and analyzing the different components that contributed to their success. For example, if I want to improve my presentation skills, I study the best speakers in the business. If I want to improve my ability to negotiate, I study the top negotiators in their fields. Borrowing the methods and attributes of highly successful people provides you with a blueprint that you can customize to serve your own needs.

I grew up in a home where competitive sports were a part of life. My father was a varsity high school basketball coach, and I had high hopes of becoming a great player. I'm happy to say that, thanks to lots of hard work, I achieved that goal.

What I most remember is logging hours of training to perfect my skills. Hours of practice can enable you to become nearly automatic—to operate on instinct—instead of having to consciously think of what to do from moment to moment—known as "muscle memory."

My dad said, "Always remember that someone else is practicing to beat you, so don't get complacent." And that's how I think of business. It's an ongoing task to fine-tune your business and strengthen your weak points because your competition is constantly striving to knock your company out of the way.

Hard work and sheer determination can often overcome a deficit of talent. Sure, your competition may appear unbeatable, but if you work hard and persevere, you'll be surprised at how much you can accomplish. Hard work does not guarantee success, but it does put you in a position to beat a more talented (even a seemingly invincible) competitor. It's vital to work with a specific goal in mind, and strive with total determination to reach it. This advice may seem like just common sense, but it's a missing ingredient for many entrepreneurs.

GROW YOUR KNOWLEDGE

Sometimes, people with college degrees behave as though they have a monopoly on knowledge and expertise. In reality, they often lack the most fundamental ingredient of all: determination. They can quote textbook theory but have no track record of real-life accomplishments.

Although it's important to get an education (I have a bachelor's degree from a university and an executive education from some of the top business schools in the country), a formal education doesn't make you an expert. Learning is a lifelong process. It doesn't end with a degree.

It's important, therefore, to be open to acquiring knowledge from every job you hold. When you're working a job you don't like, it's tempting to tune out. If you do that, however, you'll miss opportunities to grow and learn. I've held (and despised) several jobs, including waiting on tables and then working in sales for an electrical supply and pneumatics company. Even so, I picked up many valuable nuggets of knowledge at these firms.

I observed and remembered the good things and bad things, especially from my supervisors. I mostly learned what *not* to do, e.g., how *not* to treat employees. I absorbed these lessons—how my bosses acted, how they conducted meetings—and I later applied such lessons to my company in a positive way.

Although many of these lessons were negative, I did work with a few good managers—people who demonstrated what good leadership could accomplish. For example, I admired the managers who took the time to talk with me and were genuine. When they explained to the team why we did things and how we played into the company's core mission, it helped make us feel part of something. When managers treat employees with respect, it motivates them to work harder and smarter. I think what we, as leaders, sometimes don't realize is that it's the small things and quick interactions with staff that can go a long way in motivating an entire company.

Most of what I learned wasn't earth-shattering, but these small lessons have gone a long way toward helping me build a solid company with loyal and highly motivated employees.

Even if you *really* dislike your job and your bosses, scoop up as much information as you can. Then park it in a "virtual toolbox." Observe the behavior of your managers, make a note of how the company markets itself, scrutinize how meetings are conducted, analyze the company culture, and assess for yourself the effects of that culture on the attitudes and behavior of employees and customers alike.

BE A SPONGE

Don't let a negative experience keep you from gaining insights that you can later put to good use.

In addition to acquiring hands-on experience, consider working on an advanced degree or at least a continuing education course or certification program. Invest in your staff, as well: Encourage them to build their skills through company-assisted training—or help cover the costs of classes that support their jobs. This investment will produce (for you and for them) greater employee confidence, improved skills, and—ultimately—better customer service.

Schooling alone is not a substitute for experience, but neither is experience a replacement for formal education. Over time, it's the combination of both education and experience that produces optimum results.

SELF-MANAGEMENT

You can't manage others until you can manage yourself. You need to wake up on time, get to work on time—show up—then organize your workload and handle a multitude of details.

How?

First, you must get organized. Second, don't try to accomplish too many things at once. Make a list of priorities—two or three major tasks you want to accomplish—and attack those priorities right away. If you can tackle those tasks, then *you* will control the day, not vice versa.

As the leader of a company, you'll discover that it's easy to bite off more than you can chew. What's more, the old adage that "time is money" will take on a new meaning. You'll find that your time is now much more valuable than it was when you were an employee, and that the decisions you make and the actions you take will have a profound effect on your company's health and direction. That's why it's essential to use your time in efficient ways—which means, in large part, delegating lower-priority tasks to others whenever possible.

Don't try to take on the world every day. Instead, focus on those two or three "mission-critical" tasks.

Chapter Four

ORGANIZE

MONEY

Every generation of entrepreneurs has its big names– larger-than-life leaders and business models who spark admiration, inspiration, and emulation. The late 19th century had captains of industry, including John D. Rockefeller and Andrew Carnegie; the mid-20th century featured the "conglomerate kings," such as Tex Thornton and Harold Geneen; the 21st century has its Zuckerberg and Musk.

I don't blame business owners for dreaming of becoming billion dollar unicorns. Who wouldn't want to receive a massive cash infusion and become transformed overnight into a respected "player" in the business world?

It should go without saying, though, that business unicorns are extremely rare (hence the name.) The vast majority of start-ups will have to self-finance. Like me, their owners will have to bootstrap their companies from abstract concepts into realities.

Here are six tips on how to do exactly that.

1. Define your version of success. Don't fall into the trap of believing that someone else's definition of success must be yours. Your company doesn't have to be the recipient of a venture-funded windfall. It doesn't have to be featured on the cover of Forbes or Fortune. It only has to be what you want it to be.

2. Focus on sustainable profits. Some entrepreneurs seek the fast exit instead of the long slog required to build their companies. Growing a company is much more difficult than becoming a unicorn—and rarely as glamorous. It requires that you invest massive quantities of time in developing a top-quality workforce, a core mission, and a culture to which you are truly committed. For me, creating a profitable and sustainable business was the top priority. This is how the overwhelming majority of successful businesses are grown.

3. Forget about office space. In the beginning, many start-ups have no reason to lease office space. Thanks to modern technology and distributed workforces, there's never been a better time to build a bootstrapped business from your own home with minimal costs.

4. Use your own tools. Similar to #3, if you already have a functioning computer, printer, desks, filing cabinets, and other necessities, don't buy others exclusively for the business.

Focus on building the organization rather than spending money on new furniture, equipment, and supplies that you don't really need.

5. Learn to wear different hats. Learn to do things for yourself. Acquire new skills and become a jack-of-all-trades if necessary. Initially, you probably won't have the resources to hire enough people. When you're bootstrapping a business, you have to be creative. You have to take on a lot of responsibilities yourself. You may not be the ideal candidate for every position, but you'll have no choice but to learn to wear many different hats. Embrace those roles and enjoy them as best you can.

6. Defer the perks. Avoid the temptation to pay yourself an oversized salary and spend money on perks to boost your status. Your business should be the perk. If you think you need an extravagant lifestyle to be a "real" business owner, you may not be a business owner for very long. Your company should be your fun, your glamor, and your incentive to get up in the morning. That's what should get you excited and invigorated. In the beginning, gratification will have to be delayed, and frugality pursued. For a while, you may have to pay yourself almost nothing so you can reinvest the company's earnings.

One area in which it's easy to overspend is employee salaries. I'm a big believer in paying people 5 or 10 percent more than the industry average to acquire and retain top talent. During ACD's early years, however, I sometimes paid too much, which gave some people an inflated sense of their own value. I intended to pay above-market rates to encourage a superior quality of work, but some employees misinterpreted this motivation. They believed I was paying them a higher salary because they were the very best in the world and ACD was lucky to have them. In short, I sometimes got the worst of both worlds by overspending: egotistical and underperforming employees. I still believe in paying more than the market rate, but I have learned not to overdo it.

It's important to ensure that expenditures don't exceed cash flow, and even more important to place some cash in reserve. This money will serve as a safety net—a resource that can be tapped "on a rainy day."

It's also critical to develop a stellar credit history, allowing you to expand your credit lines and strengthen your banking relationships.

I've heard wannabe business owners talk about how great a business would be as a vehicle to "expense" things.

Bad idea.

First, it's not ethical. Second, it will quickly deplete your bank account.

I've heard of people who thought it was acceptable to expense equipment from a DIY store to maintain houseplants at their homes—because they included a home office. Because clients occasionally visited these home offices, they rationalized; it was okay to list these expenditures as business expenses. Not true.

Launching a business is about more—much more—than getting some dubious tax deductions or impressing your friends by treating them to free lunches.

RETAIN A GOOD ATTORNEY

Chances are good that, as a new business owner, the threat of litigation won't be one of your top concerns. But even if you are never sued, or threatened with a lawsuit, an attorney will help you with a host of projects you probably haven't antici-pated—from reviewing contracts and developing workplace policies to conducting audits of your existing practices to ensure that you're on the right side of the law.

I strongly suggest that you hire a reputable lawyer. Talk with local business leaders to obtain referrals, and interview several candidates. Don't go cheap. Choose an attorney with experience and knowledge. It's well worth investing in a quality legal advocate to protect you, your personal assets, and your company's assets. At the very least, you'll rest easier once you retain the right lawyer.

Over the years, our attorneys have handled lawsuits and contracts and patents. We've also had attorneys help us when it came to dismissing employees. Having a good lawyer can go a long way toward alleviating the stress that attends tack-ling any issue (and there are probably more than you think) with legal ramifications.

KEEP YOUR BUSINESS PLAN SIMPLE

The formal process of creating a business plan is highly over-rated. In my experience, it's better to go basic and get going. Intricate plans tend to derail action. I'm not suggesting that you don't need a game plan—you do. It's important to know your market, how your product or service fits into that market, who your competitors are, and your costs and budget. It's also important to create a basic plan. However, don't become paralyzed by technicalities. So many aspects of business change—so fast—that many goals are moving targets. A business plan should serve as a work-in-progress guide, not as Holy Scripture.

Adhering to the "orthodoxies" in overly detailed business plans causes many entrepreneurs to be too rigid in their thinking. You must be able to make fast decisions, bold moves, and be flexible at all times. If the initial idea for a product or service no longer works, be quick to twist it, bend it, or discard it in favor of something better.

If you think your business plan is going to be a permanent roadmap, think again. Once the plan makes contact with the real world, all bets are off. General Dwight Eisenhower said, "In preparing for battle, I have always found that plans are useless, but planning is indispensable." In other words, it's great to have a plan, but adaptability is far more important. Think fast, and use the best data at your disposal. Make decisions from your "gut," and you'll usually make the right decision.

Also, don't assume that effective and productive methods will remain effective and productive. Continually analyze and update those processes if needed. Are they still delivering the level of service and quality your customers expect? If not, review your models and business processes to determine how to better satisfy customers' wants and needs. (Keep in mind that customer expectations are constantly changing, especially when disruptive new players enter your industry and raise customer expectations with a new product or service.)

In addition, ask yourself: "What can I do to eliminate wasted steps, procedures, or nonessential protocols?" In some cases, you can leverage technology to automate mundane operational tasks and eliminate non-productive activities. Then, you and your staff can use the newfound time to concentrate on your company's core mission.

MAXIMIZE YOUR EFFICIENCY

Have you ever reached the end of a workday, and then realized that you accomplished nothing of real value? We've all been there. It's human nature to address the issues directly in front of us, rather than maintaining our focus on long-term goals. I used to have an out-of-control email habit, hitting my refresh button every few minutes. I've since mended my ways by scheduling regular times to check my inbox.

Technology can serve us, and it can also distract us. To maximize your productivity, it's important to minimize distractions (technology-based and otherwise) by controlling your desire to micromanage, the urge to personally address every employee or customer complaint or to attend every departmental meeting. Speaking of meetings ... most of them are significant drains on a leader's time and efficiency. In theory, they are a good vehicle for brainstorming and problem-solving. In reality, though, many are (to quote MSNBC's tagline) "a place for politics," posturing, and endless discussions about minutiae. Too often, meetings generate little or nothing of value—unless you define socializing as something of value.

I've worked for organizations that form committees whenever a cloud appears in the sky. They meet repeatedly, but rarely, if ever, make a single actionable decision. Everyone smiles and pushes critical issues to the bottom of the "to do" list.

My suggestion: save socializing for coffee breaks, lunch, or after work. Schedule meetings *only* when there is a pressing need to gather the team in one room or on a conference call. Otherwise, use the time to *act*—to physically advance your organization's most important goals.

BUILD A NETWORK OF RESOURCES

As much as we might want to bootstrap our businesses with our own resources, it's a good idea to set aside substantial capital reserves, which is sometimes beyond the means of small business owners. With this in mind, I recommend that you open a corporate checking account and establish a line of credit with a bank. It's also a good idea to build reliable relationships with insurers and (in some cases) with outside investors.

To start, choose a banker who takes an interest in your business and offers personalized services. As you grow your company through fiscally sound practices, establish a line of credit that you can tap if you experience a sudden growth spurt or if you need ready cash. *Caveat*: do not rely on the credit line for long-term financing. Instead, use the money to meet pressing needs, and pay it down as quickly as you can. This shouldn't be problematic, as long as you establish a savings account (capital reserves) in tandem with the credit line.

If your business is growing fast, consider meeting with potential investors to offer equity in the company. At ACD, we regularly receive calls and emails from prospective investors. In the beginning, I ignored these communications because I was so focused on simply building the company. As time passed, however, I took some meetings, during which, I learned quite a bit. Among other things, I learned how to "get my company in shape" for an outside partner; how to pitch the business to an investor; and most important, how to build a network of potential partners. Although you may have no interest at the moment in attracting investors, it's wise to cultivate a network of prospective "money people." That way, you'll have an interested group of people who are ready to provide investment capital if you need it.

Insurance is essential protection in a litigious society, but it's often the last thing entrepreneurs consider during the early stages of a start-up. Don't bypass insurance! Find a quality broker who will analyze your exposures and ensure that you have enough coverage to protect everything you've worked so hard to build. Consider investing in: Liability Insurance; Errors and Omissions Insurance (E&O); Directors & Officers Liability Insurance (D&O); and Employment Practices Liability Insurance (EPLI).

Chapter Five

GROW

MEASURE IT, MANAGE IT

Without relevant data, management is impossible.

Learn which key performance indicators (KPIs) are important to your business, and then measure them regularly. For example, if answering telephones is an essential indicator of the success of your business, analyze call volume during different hours of the day, the percentage of calls answered, hang-ups, and voicemails. This can help you determine the peak work hours, allocate staff more efficiently, and make all kinds of data-backed decisions.

THE 80/20 PRINCIPLE

There are many "80/20" rules, laws, and rules of thumb. For our purposes, I'm referring to the rule that states that 80 percent of your results come from 20 percent of your activities. It's not uncommon, for example, for 80 percent of revenues to come from 20 percent of customers. Hence, it makes sense to lavish special attention on the 20 percent who provide the most value to your business. I'm not suggesting that you ignore everyone else. I'm merely recommending that you deliver VIP service to the 20 percent who account for 80 percent of your revenue.

Note: When it comes to marketing and social media, it's also likely that 20 percent of your activities will yield 80 percent of your ROI. So direct your efforts toward the most effective 20 percent of social media campaigns rather than trying to "fix" the remaining 80 percent.

SACRIFICE SHORT-TERM SUCCESS

Looking to make a fast million? Here today, selling the company tomorrow?

Not me, thanks.

I believe in forming companies that will stand the test of time, create stable jobs for loyal employees, and provide customers with quality solutions (today *and* tomorrow) through ongoing innovation.

News stories of companies enjoying overnight exponential growth and selling for astronomical sums are the exception. Don't make the mistake of ignoring the long-term process of building the business—a process that requires old-fashioned hard work. Think about building the infrastructure and the culture you want to ingrain in your organization—elements that will distinguish you from the competition. Think long-term, and you'll be surprised at how fast you can grow the firm.

In the beginning, you may be tempted to accept anybody and everybody as a client. Because you haven't yet built a reputation, many prized customers will adopt a "wait and see" attitude toward your business, leaving you with relatively few choices.

Do *not* accept just anybody as a customer.

At ACD, we sacrificed some short-term success by rejecting prospective clients we considered "difficult." (Unfortunately, we did accept a few borderline cases, and believe me, we learned some hard lessons.) From a cash-flow perspective, it would have best to accept anyone with a pulse, but over the long haul, that would have been a mistake. Difficult clients tend to gobble up so much time and so many resources that the ROI is usually low. If my goal had been to make "quick money," that might have been a fair trade, but I insisted on playing the long game. I was focused on winning the 20 percent of clients who would eventually provide 80 percent of revenue. So I exercised patience, and eventually, my patience was rewarded in the form of higher-paying, lower-maintenance customers.

Another way in which I sacrificed short-term success was by continuing to own and operate the business myself. Almost from the start, I received considerable interest from private equity and venture capital firms. I could easily have issued equity in exchange for a significant cash injection. This, also, would have enhanced ACD's reputation. Oftentimes, though, customers take you more seriously when they learn that you're backed by equity financing. They tend to see you as more legitimate—as a company that's likely to last. Still, I turned away the investment capital in favor of bootstrapping the business and reinvesting the revenues.

In the end, this proved to be a very wise decision. Instead of receiving some fast cash, instead of being tempted by the prospect of immediate gratification, I retained ownership—and control—of a growing company with value that has increased dramatically.

THE IMPORTANCE OF BEING AGILE

When it comes to decisive action, many companies "just say no." Instead, they get tangled in red tape and pointless meetings.

Although meticulous planning, and even meetings, are sometimes necessary, continually waiting for the "perfect moment" to decide does not lead to explosive growth. Being nimble, acting quickly, and adjusting course along the way is a better approach than dithering over vital decisions. The best approach is to keep your mind open and make incremental changes to new products and services *after* customers "beta test" them. In short, it's important to balance agility with informed and research-based decision-making.

Many companies plan meetings, form committees, and then form more committees until they finally reach a decision. These companies are my favorite competitors because they're slow-moving. By the time our product or service is field-tested and rolled out, they're still debating catchy names and slogans for their newest offering.

Today's most competitive firms get their products to market quickly and worry about perfecting them after soliciting customer feedback.

At ACD, we know there's no way to predict every bug that will be found and every tweak that will be made. It's also impossible to anticipate every new (or previously unrecognized) problem for which a solution will be needed. Rather than fall prey to "analysis paralysis," we say: "Let's field-test a basic product. Let's get it out there, get customer feedback, and then determine how to refine it." We've done this with several top technology solutions, and some of the key features were installed *after* the products were brought to market. We got them to market fast and fine-tuned them later, and we've used this approach with some of our best-selling solutions.

As a rule, I try to set 3-month, 6-month, and 12-month goals, but not much further out than that. I sketch out a rough idea of what I'd like to accomplish during these timeframes. I schedule new product releases and new services. I plan anticipated awards, and the attendant publicity campaigns, to maximize marketing effect.

Planning ahead, but not too far ahead, lets you establish short-term and intermediate-term goals that are less likely to require drastic revision. If you plan too far in advance, the competitive landscape will probably shift, forcing you back to the drawing board. These days, the pace of business is often too fast to permit detailed planning much more than a year in advance. I'm not saying that you should limit your plans to a 12-month timeframe—only that you should keep your longer-term projects a bit more general and flexible, because you know you'll have to make adjustments.

BANISH BAD IDEAS

It's important to encourage innovation, creativity, and new ideas. At the same time, you must know when to admit failure and shut down a once-promising idea or project. The wrong idea (or the right idea at the wrong time) can jeopardize your company's financial health.

If you've tried a new idea and it doesn't seem to be working, especially if it's losing money with no end in sight, cut your losses ASAP. *If you're going to fail, fail fast.* The people who spearheaded the project might be disappointed, and even resist its termination, but the company cannot be hampered by an idea whose time has not yet come, or will never come.

More than once, ACD launched new product or service features that we hoped our clients would find valuable; but they didn't. Rather than waste more time trying to revamp the idea (because "it's a great idea, and we need to see it through to the end"), I called it quits. If I determined that the project was unnecessarily draining time, money, and/or manpower, I summoned the courage to admit failure and move on, regardless of whose feelings were hurt.

Never fall victim to the "sunk costs fallacy." In most cases, attempting to recover money that's been spent on a losing proposition by investing even more money (also known as "tossing good money after bad") will compound the original mistake.

LOST-COST, HIGH-IMPACT SOCIAL MEDIA

Question: Why promote your company and its offerings on social media?

Answer: It can be a very cost-effective way to promote product and brand awareness. In fact, an appealing and ongoing social media presence can help you effectively compete against multi-million-dollar (or even multi-billion-dollar) rivals.

The number-one challenge for a new business is building name recognition. In the real world, you must start from scratch to build an identity—and the same is true on social media. Nothing happens overnight in either the physical or the digital world, which is why, a well-constructed social media plan is important.

To start, broadly define your target market. Are you a business-to-business (B2B) or a business-to-consumer (B2C) enterprise? The answer is critical to developing an appropriate marketing plan. For example, if you own a restaurant, it would be a mistake to devote the bulk of your social media resources to LinkedIn, because it connects companies and business professionals to one another but is not a consumer focused platform. If you're a B2C company, then Facebook, Twitter, Instagram, or even Pinterest are better bets. A good social media campaign reaches the maximum number of prospective customers for the fewest dollars.

As a next step, further segment your audience by researching what the competition is doing. I'm not recommending that you spend most of the day spying on your rivals; simply observe how they promote their products, and how they build and maintain brand awareness. Which social media platforms do they use? Which audiences do they target, and what kinds of messages are they using to capture the attention of those audiences?

If your rivals have a presence on every social media platform under the sun, that doesn't mean you should do the same. In fact, it probably won't make sense for you to do that.

If a key competitor uses five different platforms, determine whether they are attracting a significant number of followers and generating a lot of buzz before you imitate their approach. *One common newbie mistake is joining multiple platforms and then failing to follow through.* The entrepreneur who actively engages people on a site for a month—or a year and then just walks away or disappears will severely damage the company's image. If you debut with a big splash on Facebook and disappear a few weeks later, it will appear to Facebook users that (A) you've gone out of business; (B) nobody is excited about your company and its products; or (C) you've gone out of business *because* nobody was excited about your company and its products. Such perceptions are common, and they're absolutely toxic to a start-up.

My advice is to limit the number of platforms, at least in the beginning, to a couple or just a handful. Choose sites that attract the highest percentage of your prospective customers, and focus your attention there before expanding to additional sites. It's better to be *very* active on one or two platforms than to establish a lackluster presence on five or six or more.

One of the best things about social media is the ability to maximize your advertising impact without spending a ton of money—or even any. Here's how.

After identifying your target audience, and choosing a few sites to reach them, decide on the goals you want to achieve. Then, craft messages that align with those goals. For example, is your goal to increase visitor traffic to your website to make direct sales? If so, your messages should include a "call to action"—an overused term that basically means "give the customer a nudge to buy, sign up, or request more info"—an online option that will prompt people to make a choice in the direction of buying from you.

In turn, your messages will help determine the type of content you should post online. Are you going to use a lot of images? Are you going to use videos? Are you going to repost articles from other people or sites, or will you post original writing, or both? Each type of content has its pros and cons.

Images: Studies have demonstrated that audiences who attend presentations that feature pictures are more likely to recall the *images* rather than the speaker's words. In such cases, a picture is literally worth a thousand words. If you decide to post photos, however, be sure they are great photos—images that are memorable and which elicit positive feelings about your business. Unprofessional photos, or ones that convey nothing in particular—particularly if you use more than a couple—will detract from your business and your overall message rather than help you.

Reposts: It's not a bad idea to occasionally repost relevant content. Unfortunately, I've seen many companies shoot themselves in the foot by doing this. Why? Because all they do is repost articles and blog posts found on the Internet. Their social media pages are nothing but an aggregation of content that's devoid of original thought or goal-oriented messaging. Essentially, they become advocates for *other people's* ideas, companies, products, and services.

Original Content: I'm a big fan of original content. It shows that you take pride in offering quality content to followers. Of course, it takes work to develop your own articles, infographics, white papers, videos, and other content. However, it doesn't have to cost much (or any) money if you produce these editorial products yourself—or, better yet, hire a skilled freelancer to create them (as opposed to a high-priced marketing communications firm).

Here are the three best types of original content to post:

1. **What's new with your company or products?** Consumers want to know what's happening. Are you releasing a new product? Are you offering a new service that will positively affect customers? Publicize developments at your firm, as well as any new products, features, benefits, or service enhancements. This is content that most people consider valuable.

2. **What's new with your people?** Did an employee just get promoted? Or run a marathon? Do you have fans who want to take a photo with you? Do you want to produce a short video about an inspirational employee or executive? This sort of content puts a human face to your organization, making it easier for consumers to relate to you.

3. **What's new in your industry?** Here's where you can display thought leadership, establishing your credentials as an industry expert or innovator. This is also a topic area that's well-suited for modified reposts. But don't just repost trend articles. Use the existing content as a springboard for commenting and analyzing the industry trends and developments. Help your fans better understand what this news means to them. It's another way to boost your credibility and position yourself as an expert in your field.

Note: When developing original content, always keep the client in mind. What does this post mean to your customers and potential customers, and why should they care? Consumers want to know *what's in it for them*, so be sure to spell it out.

How do you measure social media success?

Success means different things to different companies. For some entrepreneurs, it's measured purely by the number of hits they get. For most business owners, however, this number doesn't mean much. For example, if you're a B2B enterprise with a small target market, a fan base of several million people is worthless unless it includes lots of prospective clients. In fact, a fan base of that size might mean that your social media strategy is seriously flawed. On the other hand, if you operate an e-commerce boutique selling women's apparel, such numbers would be fantastic because each fan would represent a potential sale.

Another benchmark is how you're doing vis-à-vis the competition. Compare your social media stats with those of your closest rivals. You can use online tracking tools that will let you obtain hard data to measure the impact of your social media efforts.

Finally, don't expect a huge return on your social media investment from the get-go. There is no silver bullet. Success hinges on staying power and consistency—on communicating the right messages month after month until you reach a tipping point. The tipping point is the moment when you graduate from unknown start-up to a company people recognize and want to buy from. This is when consumers know about your pages, visit your pages, and think, "Wow! This company is full of energy; they have something interesting to say. There's two years' worth of videos and posts here. Obviously, this company's been *around* and is here to stay."

By the way, I'm sometimes asked if it makes sense to "pay to play"—i.e., to sponsor or buy online ads. That's up to you, but remember, the premise of this section is how to maximize your social media impact for a minimal cost. It couldn't hurt to conduct limited tests of sponsored or paid advertising. But if you want to keep your costs low, you may not want to spend that money—not right away.

VIDEO PROMOTIONS

People love to watch videos on their smartphones, TVs, tablets, and computers. And today, high-quality video promotions can be produced using any iPad or iPhone with a microphone. Shoot the videos with your iPhone or a camera, and then use iMovie or another editing program to create the final products.

Assuming you're the spokesperson for the company, banish any doubts or self-consciousness, and rehearse the videos until you feel at ease in front of the camera. Once that's done, you can present your business and yourself in a natural, personable way.

Next, create a few 20-second videos. As you get used to speaking on camera, feel free to produce more, but keep them short—under a minute. Otherwise, most people will switch off. Always make your points quickly, and speak with energy and enthusiasm.

Here are some more pointers:

- **Draft a rough script or outline.** Not every video has to be scripted. In fact, videos should never *come across as* scripted. However, you *will* need an outline or a rough script from which to work with unless you're a master of improvisation. (Regarding topics, stick to the list of three from the previous section: your company and its products, your people, and industry trends.)

- **Choose topics that you're passionate about.** You can't fail when you display energy, enthusiasm, and a natural-looking smile. Don't worry that you don't look or sound professional—most people are too hard on themselves. Just focus on pumping energy and excitement into your presentation. Your attitude will probably convey your message more powerfully than your words will. Often, people don't listen very carefully to what's said. Instead, they tune in to the speaker's enthusiasm. Emotions and attitude are what *really sell* you, your company, and its offerings.

- **Be genuine.** Don't act like a news anchor or a game show host. Project your own personality and energy. These days, audiences are seeking genuine people—everyday people like themselves. What they *don't* want to see are blow-dried Barbie and Ken dolls.

- **Record your rehearsals.** Buy an inexpensive stand for your smartphone, and practice, practice, practice. Just as importantly, *record* the rehearsals so you can identify weaknesses in your presentation and fix the shortcomings. (It's difficult to thoroughly analyze a performance without any "documentary evidence" to consult.) The more you practice, the better you'll get.

- **Take small steps.** People's attention spans are short and seem to be getting shorter. Most audiences want short, punchy, to-the-point videos. So my recommendation is to stay within the 30- to 60-second range. Start by creating very concise videos, and with practice, work your way up to a minute.

- **Repetition builds confidence**. With practice and repetition comes confidence. The first video you post on your Facebook page or website may not be the best you ever produce. You may *never* create one that fits your definition of "perfect," and after all, if you achieve perfection, why go on? But over time, you'll become more confident, and the quality will improve. And this confidence will carry over to other parts of your business. If you're able to make effective video presentations, you'll more effectively and *persuasively* interact with colleagues, customers, and staff.

Chapter Six

TEAM BUILDING

YOU DON'T WIN THE DERBY WITH A DONKEY

A business veteran once told me, "You don't win the derby with a donkey."

Translation: You can't build a sustainable business with third-rate employees.

In the beginning, you'll be tempted to hire anyone who's available *right now at the right price,* even if that person doesn't fit your long-term plans or even possess essential skills.

Don't do it.

Don't ever hire "good enough."

If you do, problems will arise, especially as the company expands. When you're growing a business, you need to find "good fits." You need thoroughbreds to run this race. If you select donkeys, you risk losing everything.

Even from the best employees, you'll obtain only 60 percent productivity on any given day. In reality, most employees don't work at 100 percent capacity all the time. Yes, there are those exceptional few who always work at full speed, but they're a rare breed. Most employees spend a fair amount of time socializing, surfing the Internet, and chatting about TV shows and weekend plans. That's okay. Allowing your staff a little freedom to socialize pays dividends in the form of loyalty and dedication. You may not receive 100 percent productivity, but you'll have a happier, more motivated team—one that will compensate for the downtime when it counts.

You manage a business, not a sweatshop. Treat your staff with respect. Let them take breaks and have a little fun—ensure that your business is a place where they *want* to come to work.

Hire the best people you can afford from the start, and it will pay off in the end.

Have I made the mistake of hiring donkeys? Yes, I have. On several occasions, I hired lesser-qualified or lower-priced people, which later forced me to spend more money training them. Sometimes, even that wasn't enough. Their personalities and work habits didn't mesh with the company's culture, and they had to be let go. So all those extra dollars spent on the additional training were *wasted*.

In addition to hiring qualified staff, be sure to cross-train team members so each of them can step into different roles when necessary.

The moment you rely too much on one person to perform certain tasks is the moment you become vulnerable as a company. Cross-train as many employees as possible, so you aren't reliant on a handful of "indispensable" people. You want clients to rely on your company—not one individual. A great way to do this is by working with clients on a team basis, so they recognize that your company is the sum of more than one person.

And lastly, Hire Slow and Fire Fast.

LEVERAGE TECHNOLOGY TO CREATE VIRTUAL TEAMS

Think beyond bricks and mortar.

You can field a formidable team through a virtual office environment. To create a viable team, however, you must be able to manage a geographically dispersed workforce that's well-connected and well-coordinated, and you can do this with technology.

Many social media, instant messaging, and video conferencing tools can bridge the gap between members of a remote team. Of course, this model *does* require that you trust people that you don't see on a day-to-day basis, but that needn't be a problem. Although my employees accomplish their work from home, I've found them to be very motivated and productive. The key to making this thing work is to "Trust but Verify." And you do this by developing methods to track the output of every employee.

At ACD, we use internal-tracking methods, including Slack team messaging, which enables communications between the team as a whole as well as different subgroups. In addition, we have internal controls and monitoring built into our technology platform. We're able to track when people log in to view files, how long they work on a file, how long they view a file, and how many files they look at each day. We can also monitor other key performance indicators to measure productivity. The idea is not to become Big Brother, but to learn who is performing well, which clients and partners are more demanding, and whether we're appropriately staffed at any given time. All these metrics help us analyze the health of the company and help us become more efficient and responsive.

Given some trust, the right people, and the right parameters, your team members can achieve results that often surpass those of workers who are confined to cubicles.

INCENTIVIZE YOUR TEAM

You should recognize and reward the achievements of your team members.

Many companies skimp on salaries and bonuses to cut costs, failing to realize that a happy, well-compensated employee is a more dedicated and loyal employee. Moreover, monetary compensation is not the only incentive that workers are seeking. Most also want validation and recognition for jobs well done. Toward that end, leaders should take the time to write handwritten thank-you notes, provide flexible work schedules, and find ways to make the work environment a productive and fun place.

A longtime helicopter pilot I met told me, grinning, "I get to go to work every day!" Do your employees feel like that?

At ACD, we reward team members by delivering on-the-spot bonuses to employees who do something amazing to help our clients. We also give out restaurant gift cards (worth $25 to $50), provide extra vacation days, host lunches & parties based on success, and recognize top performers through employee-of-the-month programs. We want our staff to understand that their individual triumphs translate into the success of the entire company.

Many companies also fail to invest in continuing education—a big mistake for any firm that needs a workforce with relevant, up-to-date knowledge and skills (and what firm doesn't?). At ACD, we believe that by increasing our team's job-related skills through additional training classes, school, and job development, we're improving our ability to compete. To acquire and retain the best employees, you need to pay more than the market rate—and ensure that you keep them at the top of their game.

As I mentioned earlier, however, the key is to "over-compensate" *only the top-notch candidates.* In my experience, when less-qualified workers are paid too generously, it fosters a sense of entitlement rather than enthusiasm. Reward the people who show initiative and go above and beyond. The investment in these workers will pay off many times through higher client satisfaction, repeat business, and employee retention. In the beginning, you may have trouble separating the best performers from the mediocrities, but as your company grows, both the strongest and weakest performers will stand out.

WHEN YOU HIRE THE WRONG PERSON

Let's say you've made the mistake of hiring some employees who aren't a great fit. They're not doing a bad job, but they aren't performing at the level you want. Are you doomed?

No.

There are ways to make things work, but they require both you and the employees to pull together. The first question to ask yourself is "Are these employees trainable?" If so, do you want to invest the time and money to train them? Over the years, I've made some questionable recruitment decisions, but with additional training and coaching, some of these workers became valuable contributors.

Spend time with team members who show promise, have a good attitude, are quick learners, and display genuine loyalty. If they are dedicated and sincerely thankful for the opportunity to build their careers, you have a chance to transform potential mistakes into positive outcomes. Remember: You can buy training, but not a positive attitude.

When I founded ACD, I had no experience interviewing job candidates. If someone could fog a mirror and handle the basic job description, they were hired. I also made the mistake of shuffling some employees between different positions to find the right fit when common sense showed that there *was* no good fit.

As a business owner, your mission is not to manage a rescue shelter for underachievers, so act promptly to remove the square pegs from the round holes. If someone just doesn't have what it takes, it's best to part ways sooner rather than later. Conversely, take your time during the hiring phase. Be cautious and methodical in your employee searches. Loading your team with elite performers will ensure that your company excels.

If employees can't be "rehabilitated," it's important to show compassion and understanding. If people aren't performing well, it's usually because they aren't a good fit, not because they're incompetent or lazy. They may be great people. They may even possess exceptional skills and expertise. But some people just aren't able to align with your culture, your mission, and your goals. There's nothing wrong with that, so be honest with them. As often as not, employees already know when they don't fit, and a parting of ways can be a kindness to both the employee and the business. All people want to be happy in their work, and if an employer can handle this tough situation without animosity, both parties can quickly move on.

No team is perfect. Try as hard as you want, but different personalities and levels of commitment will sometimes lead to conflict and less-than-optimal productivity. To paraphrase Carl von Clausewitz: *No human resources plan survives the first contact with reality*. Your role as a business owner is to mesh a diverse group of employees into a functioning team unit. Your job as a business leader is to encourage each team member to strive for excellence.

That said, be cautious of individuals who tout their "vast experience" with little to show for it. For example: although a salesperson may be able to claim "25 years of experience," if that person did nothing but meet the minimum requirements to survive in his last position, how much is that "experience" worth? These employees are usually the ones who cause dissension within the ranks and struggle to complete even the most basic tasks.

When hiring, look beyond the number of years logged at this or that company. Instead, look for a proven track record of growth and success, and be wary of those who boast about how great they are. Quite likely, it's all nonsense.

On a couple of occasions, we hired people who talked a good game, but couldn't perform when it came time to put rubber to the road. They were good at "spinning" their résumés and perfecting their interview skills. Too bad they didn't bring to the job that same commitment to learning, professional growth, and excellence.

Chapter Seven

LEAD

BE STEADY AND STRONG

The loss of a major account. The bankruptcy of a key supplier. The launch of a direct and well-funded competitor.

It's been a bad month.

Tough situations will arise, and as the company's leader, you must display strength and keep a steady hand on the tiller. You can't let employees become disillusioned.

People need leaders who are upbeat, confident, and inspiring—leaders who can improve everyone's resilience and morale—and their confidence in the future. It's okay (and just human) to occasionally experience moments of doubt or even despair. Just don't express those feelings publicly.

BE WILLING TO WEAR DIFFERENT HATS

Operating a small business means wearing many different hats, or functioning in a variety of roles. You'll have to know how to do every job in the company—from attracting investment to taking out the trash. No job is "beneath" a true entrepreneur. Business owners who think they're too good to answer phones are doomed to fail.

As the leader of your company, you must be able to help at every level. This demonstrates your commitment to your team and also keeps your finger on the pulses of employees, vendors, and customers. As the firm grows, you can discard some of those hats, but it never hurts to be able to jump back in to learn what's working and what isn't.

Once you're successful, however, there WILL come a time when you simply can't do it all. You'll need to delegate. Once you're on a solid growth trajectory, most of your time should be spent doing what you do best: *managing* the business (as opposed to running it directly). Hire strong, solid individuals in each department within your company as the need arises, and then outsource certain functions when you can. Try outsourcing your accounting, phone system solutions, IT support, communications development and editing, and website management. Eliminate any distractions that take your mind and time away from the core missions.

It can be difficult for Type A personalities to delegate because of their desire to always be in the driver's seat. Still, you must learn how to let go. Just be sure that the people to whom you assign pivotal tasks are dedicated and competent. Carefully handpick the people who will make critical decisions, and don't walk away from direct supervision of these subordinates until they've earned your confidence and trust.

POSITIVE ENERGY IS CONTAGIOUS

Enthusiasm, excitement, and a positive environment will fuel your company's success.

Most people who know me call me "hyper" and "exuberant." I speak fast, and I'm full of excitement for what I do. I mean, why do anything if you're not fired up about it?

I'm a big believer in throwing the energy you have into everything you do. Don't proceed with a project unless you're ready to give it all you can.

Mistakes will be made along the way, but if you maintain an optimistic, energized attitude, this will encourage your team to conduct their work with intensity, too.

> Hang onto the "start-up hunger" that motivated you during the early phases—the combination of desire and fear that made you feel as though you were one client away from winning or losing it all.

People want to be around friendly, positive people. If the company is a fun, forward-thinking place to work, your employees will feel valued, energized, and fired up to succeed—for themselves and as team members *and* for the company.

One key to generating enthusiasm is to never let your start-up drive fade away. When launching a new business, you'll be ready to conquer the world. But for many entrepreneurs, this drive fades when reality sets in or if success produces overconfidence. Overconfidence can sap the drive of many companies, leaving them vulnerable to savvy competitors.

Hang onto the "start-up hunger" that motivated you during the early phases—the combination of desire and fear that made you feel as though you were one client away from winning or losing it all.

Complacency is the enemy—something that can easily fuel the collapse of your company.

Another key is to inspire your team with a vision. Paint this vision by giving your company a core identity that is larger than any single individual or single project. Construct a vision that everyone believes in and is committed to—every day.

At ACD, we're committed to superior service. Everything we do must give our clients a more satisfying experience. By providing them with the tools, training, support, and teamwork to be successful, our mission is also to help each and every team member grow and take ownership of their jobs and careers.

Chapter Eight

SELL

GET, GROW, & RETAIN

The cost of acquiring new clients is always higher than the cost of retaining existing clients. For this reason, I focus on three simple words: Obtain, Grow, and Retain. Once you (A) acquire a new client, it should be your goal to (B) expand the number of solutions you sell to that customer; and (C) retain them with superior service. In theory, it's not complicated. However, many companies fail to Grow and Retain thanks to sporadic client follow-up or even apathy.

Don't spend most of your time chasing new business when concentrating on your current customers can reap amazing benefits.

Work hard to maintain the clients you have by demonstrating that you value their business. Maintain continuous communications with them, and (I can't stress this enough) *deliver superior service.*

You may have a great product or service, but if your customer relations suffer, so will your business. Excellent customer service is something that all businesses should provide, and it starts with the act of answering the phone. Shirking this basic function is the first step toward failure. Your staff members need to answer the phones quickly and cheerfully while maintaining a sympathetic, helpful attitude. The clients are on the phone because they need your assistance and want a reassuring, knowledgeable, and comforting service rep. The caller may be placing an order, asking a question, expressing a concern, or merely establishing a personal connection with you. Whatever the reason, each call is an opportunity to make your company stand out.

When starting a business, it may be necessary to work with clients who are less than desirable. In fact, the reason some clients will choose you is because nobody else wants to work with these difficult and demanding companies—also known as "PITA" (Pain in the Ass) clients.

The first clients you attract are likely to treat you rudely, pay poorly, and make unreasonable demands. One of our first clients had a manager who was condescending and arrogant—a bona fide jerk. Although the client represented more than half of our income, I had to take the bold step of "firing" them. Clients who drain your energy, who view you as merely a servant (and not a partner), will not only limit your growth, but may also prevent you from obtaining clients who *will* value your services. It's tough, but pruning the dead wood is good for you and your company. One step backward sometimes results in two leaps forward.

Although you may acquire a substantial number of PITAs during the start-up phase, don't tie the future of your company to them. Occasionally, some of these companies may become solid citizens once they come to appreciate the value that you deliver. But most will never fully appreciate your efforts, and eventually, their business will no longer be worth the time, effort, and cost. As your company grows and builds its reputation, it will be easier to attract top-tier clients. Once you acquire a critical mass of A-List customers, gradually fire the PITAs in favor of organizations that match your ideal client profile.

FLAWLESS, FAST, AND FREE

Customers want your product or service to be all three.

We work hard to honor the first two wishes, but we can't accommodate the third.

Our society is now characterized by short attention spans and a desire for instant gratification. This is why outstanding customer service is essential. You can't give away your wares, but you can easily add more value to your products or services to help them stand out. Adding value can be *the* game changer in your industry. If you have something valuable to offer, many customers will pay a higher price. It's only when you fail to demonstrate sufficient value that price becomes an issue.

Every business sells a product or service, yet nobody wants to be "sold" anything. We hate being pitched to and pressured to buy. We like to be the ones who control the when, where, and how we purchase something based on our personal preferences.

So how can you sell without annoying people? The answer is to present the *value* of your product or service, and then allow prospective customers to decide if, when, and how to take advantage of that value. Be enthusiastic, cheerful, and genuinely excited about your service or product, and those emotions will become infectious. When you focus on the value that you provide, and customers believe that value is genuine, this will "sell" your offerings. When customers believe your solution is *the solution*, it will be difficult for them to say no.

By the way: one of the most overlooked forms of communication these days is the old-fashioned, handwritten letter. Today, people send a quick text or email, but they don't have as much impact as a handwritten note. I advocate handwritten cards as a program of customer appreciation to retain clients and let them know you care. This doesn't have to cost much. It merely requires you to be creative, consistent, and caring. Thoughtfulness counts most when you are giving clients your time and attention, so make the effort to customize your letters. A personal touch lets them know they are valued.

PERCEPTION VS. REALITY

"I'm doing a great job. My customers love me."

Do they?

In general, you may be doing a great job, but if minor problems arise, and they aren't resolved promptly, customers will form a negative opinion of your firm, despite otherwise exceptional service. Don't let them draw an incorrect conclusion when they're on the receiving end of a glitch in your system. Display genuine concern and help them solve any problems— *fast*.

Some people believe their clients are happy if they don't hear anything from them.

Wrong.

Too often, no news is bad news.

At ACD, our client-care and quality-assurance teams are always checking in with clients to ensure that everything is going well. During the course of these check-ins, they sometimes discover minor issues—"molehills" that could easily grow into "mountains" if ignored. For example, we once discovered that a customer was unhappy because of the emails they were receiving from us. We assumed they would want to be updated about anything and everything, but we assumed wrongly. For them, our regular notifications were a nuisance. So we adjusted our customer-service settings to make sure they would no longer receive so many routine communications. Had we continued to assume they were satisfied, they might have stewed in silence until they couldn't take it anymore. In fact, they told our service representative that if we hadn't changed course, they were planning to fire us.

Stay in touch with your customers to make sure that they're happy. Don't assume they're happy because they aren't complaining. The vast majority of dissatisfied customers will never say a word to you. They'll just leave.

MANAGE YOUR SALES TEAM

One of the toughest things about running a company is managing your sales team. Sales fuel the growth and success of a company, but if the team is disorganized or inconsistent, your results will suffer, and worse yet, you'll have a tough time staying in business.

This may sound like a massive generalization, but salespeople seem to operate with an extreme mindset. They are either super motivated or they seem to want to hide and do absolutely nothing. It's either one or the other. Over the years, very few I've ever met are super motivated. The key to managing a sales team is to have clearly defined sales goals and metrics to measure results. I have failed in this area many times throughout the years because I trusted and was "sold" by my own sales team that everything was under control, only to find out they weren't doing much of anything.

I've made the mistake of paying some salespeople **way too high** a base salary, which left them comfortable and unmotivated to sell. Others simply used their stay with my company as a "layover" to gain some technology sales experience to move quickly on to another job or even complete their MBA as a side project using our organization as their "case study." I even had one guy use a travel trip to go to an interview with a competitor on my dime! Crazy huh?

Yes, they took advantage of my niceness. Did I allow it? I guess. So moving forward, this is what I put in place for sales success

1. Sales representatives have a low base, high commission opportunity.
2. Have defined sales goals and metrics that must be met quarterly.
3. Sales teams must document and record all sales activity daily.

4. Our accounting team must approve all travel, and every contact they are meeting is documented. Their trips and meetings times are all on the calendar.
5. The sales pipeline must be growing at all times.

I dislike micromanaging, but when it comes to sales, it pays to monitor and demand results. A hands-off approach in this area has been a personal failure of mine, and I had to step in and take control. Don't let your sales process get out of hand.

Chapter Nine

WIN

KNOW THE COMPETITION

Launching a business without knowing the strengths and weaknesses of your competition is like jumping into shark-filled ocean slathered in sardine oil.

When I study my competition, I especially focus on how they portray themselves within the industry and to their target markets. I observe what they say about themselves in their ad campaigns and social media. Which solutions are they pushing? Which selling points are they touting? How are they trying to distinguish themselves from competitors like me?

> Your job isn't to copy the competition. It's to learn enough about them to beat them.

Gathering such information helps me understand how to counter those messages. It also provides a better idea of why customers would want to buy from ACD. In addition, studying what's worked for my competitors, and what hasn't, helps me create more effective sales and marketing plans. Among other things, this research offers me real-life case histories that are as good (and often more relevant) than anything I could study at a business school.

Be diligent in your research, but don't become obsessive about the competition. When I say diligent, I mean that you should routinely check out the competition to see what they're doing. When I say obsessive, I mean that you can't spend all your time reading every social media post made by competing companies. This would take your eye off a core goal, which is improving *your* business. Your job isn't to copy the competition. It's to learn enough about them to beat them. You need to strike a balance between focusing on your company and learning just enough about the competition to ensure that you're always one step ahead.

I'm a former collegiate basketball player, and because of my competitive spirit, I view business through the lens of sports. I'm also an amateur historian who enjoys studying military history. Although nothing compares to the seriousness of war, I view my company as locked in a titanic struggle to beat superior opponents. If you view business the same way, you will compete with a warrior's zeal. Study your opponent's weaknesses, and strategize to overcome their control of the market.

Be vigilant—even a little paranoid—and don't be caught napping. Monitor your industry's trends and stay informed on what your competitors are doing.

It's okay to be *a little* paranoid. Otherwise, you'll be left in a cloud of dust. By no means, however, do I suggest spending your time looking for black helicopters painted with your competitor's logos. Just be tuned in and ready to react decisively to a rapidly changing marketplace.

APPEAR LARGER THAN LIFE

Competitors used to say that our company was all smoke and mirrors because we were based from home offices. Well, so was Steve Jobs.

It's not *where* you work, but the quality of the services or products that you deliver.

Even so, it can be helpful to appear larger than life—certainly larger than you really are. Promote yourself and the company with high-quality marketing materials, a website, and social media campaigns. Give the appearance of the company you hope to be in 10 or 15 years. Doing so will help you create a larger-than-life image at virtually no cost. Remember, you'll be competing, in some cases, against multi-billion-dollar companies with legions of sales and marketing professionals. Run lean, but don't *look* like you're running lean.

THE SUCCESS MINDSET

One frequently overlooked key to success is "The Success Mindset"—a worldview that combines an action-orientation, with a desire to learn, with a fierce competitive drive. Mix these elements together, and you get MOMENTUM.

Newton's first law of motion states that *an object at rest stays at rest, and an object in motion stays in motion unless it's acted upon by an unbalanced force.* In other words, once you take action—once you start to generate momentum—it's easy to keep that momentum going almost indefinitely. (Sometimes the hard part is getting started.)

Be action-oriented. Harness the proactive, not reactive, form of action. Many people have great ideas, but do nothing to transform the ideas into realities. Woody Allen once said that 80 percent of success is showing up. I agree. In my experience, imagining a great new idea gets you 20 percent of the way there. The remaining 80 percent of the equation is "showing up" (taking action) to make it happen.

Be a zealous learner. Be an open mind. Be someone who soaks up bits and pieces of knowledge for use in future situations. Read. Take classes. Study on your own. There's always something to learn. Admit that you don't know everything and *never will* know everything. Don't let success fuel arrogance. Just because your company is profitable, or you've earned an MBA or a Ph.D. doesn't mean that it's time to take a lifelong mental vacation. There's always somebody who knows more—someone from whom you can learn.

Exude energy and a competitive drive. Let your energy flow to everyone around you. I believe that excitement and energy are contagious. If you're excited about what you're doing—if you display fire, drive, and commitment—you can't help but inspire your colleagues, employees, prospective employees, and customers.

To become genuinely excited, though, you must relish the fight. You must enjoy the competitive challenge of running a business. To fuel your competitive drive, it helps to adopt an underdog mentality—to view yourself as a David facing an arena of Goliaths. These giants are better-funded and often have more skilled and talented people on their side. Your only weapons are resourcefulness, tenacity, and a willingness to work harder. These attributes, however, will quickly dissipate unless you constantly inspire, energize, and re-energize your team to charge into that arena day after day, month after month.

You have to enjoy the preparation, the sweat, the hard work, and the practice. You have to be focused on constant improvement, knowing that you need to be better. You can never be satisfied that you've "made it." *The moment you think you've made it is the moment you've failed.* The moment you become complacent is the moment that a Goliath will knock your block off.

Ultimately, I believe the "secret" to business success is quite simple. It's like pushing a cart up a mountain. If you push the cart a little farther every day, you'll eventually reach your goals, after which, you'll need to set new goals. But if you ever let go—if you fail to set new goals or spend too much time congratulating yourself on your success to date—the cart will roll down the mountain to where you started, or even beyond.

The lesson? Don't *ever* stop driving forward or let off the gas. Keep your momentum going.

Chapter Ten

BONUS

THE PERILS OF TRYING TO MOTIVATE EMPLOYEES

I've long believed that the best way to motivate employees is to treat them well. I pay my employees above-average salaries, reward good performances, and provide plenty of perks.

I do this because I know what it's like to be underpaid and underappreciated, and how this can erode employee morale.

My Goal: Build a Better Culture

Back when I was a "cubicle jockey," I promised myself that when I launched my own company, it would be an inviting place to work. Instead of an oppressive and stressful environment—like those of my previous employers—I would build a relaxed and flexible culture that encouraged innovation, rewarded productivity, and allowed people to rise on their own merits. In exchange for higher pay and benefits, I would expect my employees to deliver maximum effort.

Today, my company is a reality, and I fulfilled my promise to treat employees well.

In addition to generous pay and healthcare benefits, we contribute three percent of every employee's salary to their 401(k) plan—even if they choose not to fund the plan themselves. We give bonuses when the company is doing well, as well as monthly performance-based bonuses. We provide snacks and other food and throw birthday parties and luncheons. The work environment is nontraditional (open space), and people are given the flexibility to take breaks whenever they want.

We don't ask people to "look busy." Appearances don't matter. Results do. If someone wants to take an hour-long lunch to walk in the woods to clear his or her head, that's fine. We aren't standing by the door with a watch to see if they are a minute late.

Mistaking Good Treatment for Weakness

Unfortunately, I've learned the hard way that some employees will mistake good treatment for weakness.

For example, several young employees recently approached me bearing a list of demands. They said, "Ernie, you give us a lot of stuff—food, parties, etc.—and that's great. But that's not enough. We want more. We want more awards and bigger rewards," including Netflix, game tables, massages, grocery cards, and daily feedback awards with monetary bonuses.

I thought they were joking, but they weren't. We're trying to run a technology and services company—not an adult daycare facility or a spa.

Perplexed by this encounter, I asked several friends for advice. Their response was that I had become too accessible to employees. Because I hadn't set boundaries, everyone on the team felt comfortable bypassing their supervisors and coming straight to me with complaints and demands. If a worker were told that he didn't yet qualify for a raise or promotion, he wouldn't hesitate to march into my office in an effort to extract a *yes* from "daddy" after "mommy" said *no*.

3 Valuable Lessons

Not many people behave this way, but enough *have* done it to teach me three valuable lessons.

1. Although most employees respond positively to financial and other incentives, a certain subset always mistake good treatment for weakness. Some people respond to generosity by developing a sense of entitlement.
2. It's important to establish a chain of command—and stick to it. If workers believe that they can overturn their supervisors' decisions by going straight to senior management, organizational structures and boundaries may start to collapse. If you don't follow a strict chain of command, political game-playing (and ridiculous demands) may ensue.
3. Performance incentives are a good thing but recognize that some employees will never be satisfied. You simply can't please all employees all the time. What's more, the kind of employee who responds best to incentives is usually someone who is self-motivated to begin with. Therefore, it pays to hire only self-starters with realistic expectations, and screen out anyone who shows signs of entitlement.

In my experience, the best employees will thrive in a flexible environment that offers lots of rewards. They will harness that flexibility to enhance their creativity and productivity instead of finding new ways to goof off. They will respond to bonuses by searching for ways to help the company instead of searching for ways to squeeze the company for more.

The trick, of course, is learning to distinguish the good employees from the entitled ones before they are even hired.

GOING FROM ZERO TO $20M

Building a company is hard work, a little luck, and a combination of so many different factors that make success a mystery to many. In the news, everyone sees the venture-funded firms artificially enhanced with an injection of cash, which often gives the "impression" of success while their financials and balance sheet often tell a completely different story.

This leaves the average small business owner or budding entrepreneur without a realistic perception of what it really takes to build a company from the ground up, which is the way most businesses start.

Here's a quick synopsis of what it's like at each stage of growth and what you might expect.

1. Founding to $1M

This is the stage where you wear all the hats. You work all hours, are fired up, and you are driving hard at a level you could never imagine. You love the challenge. You hire some people, maybe too quickly, but you figure if they can answer a phone and do some basic tasks, you're happy. You also may not be paying much in salaries so you can't afford the high-est-level people. You enlist family, friends on a part-time or project basis, and you are thinking of every way you can to keep costs low and reinvest everything back into your company. You are likely not taking a salary, or if you are paying yourself, it's far below minimum wage. During this time, you may forget to document meetings, keep documents, and can be a little scattered, as you don't have all the policies and procedures in place. Every client you have and every transaction hinges on every interaction. You end up taking on clients you shouldn't who are highly demanding and rude, yet you suck it up as you have to gain business. Usually, the toughest clients are your first ones. This is the "all hands on deck" stage, and everything is about building a company that is viable. It's fun, stressful, tiring, yet exhilarating. Every little win is cause for celebration.

2. $1M to 5M

Now that you've broken the $1M barrier, it's cause for celebration. You made it past a barrier many companies never do. It's a huge accomplishment but no time to rest. Your company is now in a successful stage where you feel like you have some momentum. You begin to hire more staff, and you might start to see that that your original staff are not a sharp as the new talent. Basically, you are outgrowing the skills of the first-level team. This is where you have to decide to keep them and elevate their game or let them go. You are now starting to pay yourself a fairly decent salary, but still nothing extravagant, and reinvestment is still key. You now have some respect so you can afford to "fire the bad" client.

You might, though, be in danger of having just 1 or 2 large clients and a few smaller ones, but the big ones you rely upon have control over you. You have to strive to diversify your client base so you aren't reliant on any one client. Many companies are happy to just stay in this range and make a decent living. This is the time you need to start instituting good policies and procedures and build your infrastructure for growth. If you don't and grow too rapidly, you will have a mess of disorganization. You may be able to get a credit line or loan, but you will be personally guaranteeing it. You are now making some "big decisions". The thought of delegating become a necessity, and you may start to relinquish some duties. Your accounting software for a small business might not be enough, and you may have to start thinking about graduating to a larger CPA or accounting firm. The fly by the seat of your pants days are ending.

3. $5M to $10M

This is where the wheels can come off causing you to fly off the rails. You may delegate to managers and be removed from day to day a bit more. You find it hard to step back but you start to. Your staff that was originally there sees and hears less from you and feels sad that the company is losing the family feel. You can't be that close-knit family anymore. You have fired employees, and it's tough. You might feel bad, but you have to do what's best for the company. This is when people who think they knew you well, who have fallen away from the inner circle, become disgruntled. You have to be firm and focused and realize that you are now running a bigger company, and the culture has to change. You are growing up and wearing your big boy or big girl pants now. You may have won some awards, recognition, and have some access to capital. This might allow you to secure a larger bank loan and even have the responsibilities of office space. You now need to elevate your accounting to a top quality team. The days of the bookkeeper are gone. You now have VC and equity firms calling relentlessly and hugely interested if you've attained some recognition. You start to feel successful, but you haven't made it. You can't take your eye off the ball. At this time, expect to have a lawsuit or two filed against you, an audit from a state agency and A LOT of stress wrapped in one. You might feel like the world is against you, but you can survive. You have to keep your focus and ensure only top people are leading your company. Putting in the wrong manager can drastically lead the company away from your core vision, so delegate, but not too much.

4. $10M to $20M

Now that you've broken the $10M barrier, you've now achieved another level of success!! Celebrate! But like I said before. Success is only temporary. You can't let up. Now you have some scar tissue. You are stronger mentally. You've weathered the storm and are much less emotional to employee drama. You are starting to be the grizzled leader of a real company. Business decisions are now that. Business decisions. You make them for the best of the company and move on with little emotion. You are looking for ways to innovate and now entrench your company's success even more. This is where your focus must be. Gain market share, refine your processes, internal and external. Make each department super efficient and ensure they are dialed in. You are now hiring for only the best. Those who aren't good enough don't make it through the interview process. You might be taking meetings with VC and equity partners to really become educated on the whole process and practice your pitches. You now become very savvy to the complete investment process and start to wonder whether giving up ownership and equity makes sense. You weigh the options and start thinking, but you have to keep the company moving forward, otherwise, if you are not growing, the investors lose interest. At this point, you can make a great living, have a solid company, and can choose a path that's right for you. The investment route or the evergreen route. Investment may accelerate your growth, but you are giving up control to a large extent. The company with investors backing you would aggressively push for 5x growth or more and place more demands on your leadership. The evergreen route is likely slower and less glamorous, but it is not a bad one either. It may be more stable. You could still reach your goal of $50M. Would you rather drink from a fire hose or take sips along the way. That's kind of a comparison. In the end, it's up to your own risk tolerance, goals, and personal mission.

THE FOUR DUMBEST THINGS I DID AS CEO

The biggest challenge for any startup CEO or founder is realizing how much you really don't know and how many mistakes you'll actually make.

See, when you are starting out, you're full of energy, everyone you bring aboard is excited about the mission, and you begin to delegate and trust people in various areas that are vital to your company success. Mistakes, though, unfortunately can be made as you begin the process of scaling up. When you are moving fast, these mistakes can pile up. Many could even take years to uncover, but don't fear, I'm going to give you five key mistakes I made so you don't have to.

1. **Paying staff far beyond market rate.** Call it naïve, but I inherently look for the best in people. I assume they want to do well, work hard, and be team players. My core belief hasn't changed, however, when I started the company, I believed that if I could pay people far above the going rate for their job position, it would create loyalty and lead to amazing performance. Oh, how I was wrong. I would say it backfired 75% of the time. What I got were employees who gained super inflated opinions of themselves, became lazy, and demanded even more. My advice is to pay your staff above market, treat them well but only reward those who truly perform.

2. **Allowing executive single points of failure.** Another big mistake is allowing an executive in a key department to be a single point of failure. True leaders and executives who are confident in themselves want open communication and don't control key knowledge. Those who lack leadership capabilities hide information and keep secrets. This allows them to preserve their job and use this as "leverage." The moment you have a person begin to imply they are the only person who can do a certain task and nobody else is given access to learn, you have a big problem. You have a weak link that must be addressed.

3. **Beware of the superhero hire.** We all want those super-heroes that can come in and suddenly transform your company from a contender into a champion. There are times you will hear about, or know of, supposedly successful people at other companies, and you say to yourself, if we had that person on our team, we'd be in great shape. Careful what you wish for because, inevitably, they might be knocking on your door. Your instinct will be to scoop them up and hire them fast. My advice is to slow down and really think about it. Most of the time, the one you put all your hopes in never delivers. All hype and no results.

4. **Giving out glory titles.** This is one of the mistakes many companies have. Everyone gets a title when you are small, and suddenly, you have all executives and no doers. I don't see titles as meaning much of anything in reality. Results are what matter. Just because somebody is head of customer service, don't bestow them with Chief Client Officer. An accountant doesn't have to be Chief Financial Officer, and a developer doesn't have to be called Chief Technology Officer.

It goes for director titles, too. You have to refrain from giving out titles too early. The instinct is use titles to build a "credibility" in the marketplace, but in reality, nobody cares, including your clients. Unfortunately, though, those given the big titles that don't really fulfill the role become the unqualified team members you eventually have to replace with true leaders.

So, in closing, just remember, you'll make mistakes, you'll be too nice, and some will see your energy and enthusiasm to build a great company as an opportunity to latch on to a good thing. But keep your guard up and really think before making fast decisions in these four key areas. It will help you in the long run and make it easier for your future growth.

WHAT TO LOOK FOR WHEN HIRING A CTO

What's the first image that comes to mind when you think of tech professionals?

Is it the hyper-casual Zuckerberg-style entrepreneur dressed in a hoodie, sweatshirt, and jeans? Is it the socially awkward "man-child" from shows like *Silicon Valley*? Both?

Even within the industry itself, many people stereotype "techies" as skateboard-wielding geeks with "beautiful minds" but no communication, business, or social skills.

To build a successful tech company, however, you must banish such stereotypes in favor of a real-life CTO who can drive your company's vision forward with his or her leadership skills. To that end, below are 5 tips on what to look for in a CTO:

1. **They have to be great communicators.** A CTO has to work closely with the CEO and leadership team to develop new business. To accomplish this, they must be client-facing people who inspire prospective customers and employees with their charisma and powers of persuasion. Many tech people isolate themselves from others. It's your mission to find someone who won't do that—someone who can effectively communicate to both internal and external stakeholders.

2. **They need to present professionally.** Although some CTO candidates like to convey the chic, millennial, start-up flavor by strolling through the workplace in shorts and flip-flops, the best CTOs exude a more "classical" image. They dress in professional business attire and carry themselves as executives. The Ping-Pong playing managers of unicorn companies are the exception, not the rule. Don't make the mistake of hiring someone whose appearance and demeanor will be a liability with most clients.

3. **They should be true team players and business partners.** As companies grow, it's not unusual for some CTOs to become prima donnas. Success sometimes fuels bigger egos. This is illustrated by how some of them treat other employees—as unintelligent, highly dispensable drones. By contrast, a good CTO is a genuine team player with the other employees, and a reliable partner to senior management. This cooperative spirit is what enables a company to function like a well-oiled machine—one in which every department works to deliver creative solutions to clients.

4. **They must have great managerial skills and leadership abilities.** You want a CTO who can manage every process in their department, not a glorified programmer or hacker. You want someone who's top-notch—someone who hires the best available talent instead of their friends and college roommates. From creating and implementing security policies to assisting with new business development, you want a high-tech "Renaissance Man" (or woman).

5. **They need to have a big-picture perspective.** They cannot be the tech geek who isolates themselves from the rest of the company. They need to understand how their department and their work should be integrated into the whole. They must also understand the firm's core business and mission and how they fit into that. If they're on an island removed from everyone else in the company, they will lose sight of all that.

I strongly suggest that you not hire someone with poor leadership and organizational skills—someone who's little more than a programmer with the title of CTO. All too often, especially during the start-up phase, this title is bestowed on people who show the best programming or coding skills, not the best leadership and management skills.

Chapter Eleven

Q & A: ASK ERNIE B.

WHAT SHOULD YOU KNOW BEFORE STARTING?

Building a business is going to take a lot of effort. I think most people underestimate how much work it will truly take to be successful and quit when they begin to experience adversity.

If you are truly committed to being an entrepreneur, you need to focus on a good niche in a market you can excel, and become the absolute best in that area. Another key tip is that you better make sure your clients can see your enthusiasm and commitment to delivering a top-quality product, because when the dust settles, you have to deliver results that matter to them.

What are the two most important qualities of an entrepreneur's mindset?

You need:

1. Perseverance to keep pushing forward. Most people quit when they encounter obstacles.
2. Ability to bring authentic passion and energy to your company's product or solution.

The key to being an entrepreneur is that your mindset has to be one of focus on your goal of building a successful company. You need to embody your company's brand and bring energy and enthusiasm to it. There will be a lot of challenges, and your job will be to inspire those around you. You have to keep positive momentum going when others around you have doubt or lose energy.

As a new CEO, there are many things you have to learn. Much of them by simply just doing. I could make a long list, but here's three that are key.

WHAT ARE THE MOST IMPORTANT SKILLS A YOUNG CEO NEEDS TO LEARN?

1. **How to manage people and lead.** Inspiring and rallying people around a shared mission and managing different personalities is a challenging job. You can have the greatest idea, product, or service, but if you can't lead a team, you'll struggle. It's really worth investing time into learning and studying about leadership and management.

2. **Know your numbers.** You have to know how to read a balance sheet and understand your numbers. If you don't know this key data, you won't be in business long.

3. **How to inspire people.** This is beyond just leadership. You have to bring an enthusiasm and energy to the job that can get everyone around you motivated to succeed. This energy can help your team drive forward even in tough times.

WHY SHOULD YOU STICK TO YOUR JOB AND NEVER START A BUSINESS?

I love helping new entrepreneurs, and I encourage people to get out and take that leap to start a business, but the reality is, not everyone is suited to be an entrepreneur and run a company.

It's stressful, it's hard, and requires a personality that is willing to take risk and sacrifice in a lot of different areas.

Many great and successful people who do amazing things never went out and started a business. Being an entrepreneur doesn't make certain people better than others. We all have to look inside ourselves and discover what our true calling is. Starting a business might not be on everyone's list, and you know what? That's okay.

DO ENTREPRENEURS NEED TO STUDY?

Here's the deal. Yes, you need to study to be a successful entrepreneur, but there's a point you have to take action. You can't count on "academia" to make you successful. I know many people who have degrees but lack the skill and adaptability to build and grow a company.

If you rely solely on college to educate you on business, you'll be in for a big shock when you try to build a business. I love education and come from a family of teachers and have a degree too. However, nothing I learned in college prepared me to become an entrepreneur. You learn book knowledge, not practical business skills.

To get out and take the leap to become a successful entrepreneur, it had to come from my internal drive. Degrees and education provide you tools but don't guarantee success.

It's, actually, really simple, just embrace the fact that life is about learning, growing, and continually improving your skills and knowledge. There is never a point you should ever stop building skills, but often, those skills are built by taking action, learning along the way, and driving forward.

Remember, there is no exact formula for success that works for everyone. You have to learn from other successful people, learn by doing, and create your own unique recipe.

WHAT BOOK WOULD YOU RECOMMEND TO A CEO OF A COMPANY LOOKING TO MANAGE THEIR LEADERSHIP TEAM?

I think one quick and easy book to read would be "The One Minute Manager Meets The Monkey." It will open your eyes. Too often, as a CEO, you end up taking on so many people's problems at the expense of getting your core mission done.

Before you know it, your own team is managing you as they toss their problems on your back and then check up on you to see if you are getting their job done. Before you know it, you'll be overwhelmed.

Worth a quick read. **The One Minute Manager Meets the Monkey: by Ken Blanchard, William Oncken Jr., Hal Burrows**

DID YOU HAVE A MENTOR BEFORE YOU STARTED YOUR COMPANY?

Prior to building my company, I didn't have any specific mentors. What I focused on during my "pre" entrepreneur years was reading and studying as much as I could about successful business leaders, management, leadership, sales, and business.

Once I launched my company, I did meet a former university professor/business person who consulted with me for about six years. Some colleges have former faculty or connections that they can put you in touch with that may available for consulting. It is nice to be able to bounce ideas off someone who has been where you have and get feedback. I think it's great if you can find an experienced business veteran as it can help you navigate some of the unknown waters.

I picked up some really good nuggets, that at the time, when working with my consultant, I didn't really understand but have now made sense, and I've since put into practice.

WHAT COULD BE THE CHALLENGES OF STARTING YOUR OWN COMPANY? I'VE BEEN AT A JOB FOR 10 YEARS BUT NOT GOING ANYWHERE?

I was in your same position. I was stuck in a job with no mobility and knew that the only way to succeed in my dreams would be to take that entrepreneurial leap. In my situation, my wife and I sold our house and lived off our savings for a year as we bootstrapped our company.

Here are a few challenges you'll have to handle:

1. **Are you going to have business partners?** If you do, choose wisely and make sure they are willing to put skin in the game.

2. **Making sure your product or service is the best in a competitive market.** You have to focus intently on truly having something that is great and people are willing to pay for.

3. **How you are going to build a reputation when you have none?** You have to get that first client, which is very tough. Once you do, though, they can become a great advocate for you.

4. **Do you have the ability to persevere even when told NO by many potential clients?** You'll run into many of these NOs, as most customers are weary at first of new businesses.

5. **People.** If you are going to have employees, eventually, you'll have to learn how to manage. If you can't lead people and inspire them, you won't be successful.

6. **Knowing your numbers.** Once you get your company going, you need to know key financial metrics, how to read a profit & loss statement, etc. Know your numbers

7. **Obscurity.** Probably one of the biggest challenges. Most people underestimate how hard it is to get your "name"

out there as a company. You can have the greatest product or service but getting customers to know who you are is a major challenge, especially in a world of so much marketing "noise." The good news, though, if you have a niche, your market is much more focused.

HOW DO I STAY WITH ONLY ONE BUSINESS IDEA AND WORK IT?

Simple. You have to have an unwavering level of focus. If you don't have focus, you will constantly be looking for other ideas, you'll neglect the process of truly seeing your idea through and building a company.

Just remember, becoming an entrepreneur or building a company has NO guarantee of success. There is no perfect company you will ever build. All you can do is do the preparation work that's required and set yourself up to be in the best position to succeed.

So if you have an idea and you think it's good... prepare, plan, focus, and execute. Success will be determined by all of that and whether the market sees your product or solution as something that's wanted.

HOW DOES A CEO/FOUNDER/OWNER PICK THEIR SALARY?

It's not really a matter of picking, at first. It's a matter of creating a company that generates income first and foremost.

When you are starting out in a bootstrapped company as CEO/Founder, don't expect to make anything at first. You have to be willing to forgo any pay until your company can be cash flow positive. Even then, you have to temper your excitement and reinvest most of the money back into the company. The reality is that, in the early years, you will have to pay yourself very little or just enough to get by until you can truly turn your company into a viable business. The title of CEO, in reality, isn't that glamorous and comes with a ton of responsibility when you are the one putting your house, assets, and money on the line to keep your business going.

Too many start-up entrepreneurs can get into the mindset that they can pay themselves whatever they want. This is completely wrong thinking as the company must come first. If the company fails, there's nothing to pay anyone.

My best advice is to pay yourself just enough to get by once you are able to take a paycheck, and then focus intently on building a "real" solid company that can eventually allow you to take the realistic pay you thinking about.

WHAT ARE THE BEST TRICKS TO OVERCOME LAZINESS?

People, in general, naturally look for the easy way. Hard work and effort take discipline. So how do you overcome the inherent state of laziness that many have? You build discipline. The simple adage of work before play.

Here are 5 things I personally do:

1. I have goals to accomplish every day, and I start by writing them down. Make them realistic.
2. I ensure I tackle the biggest one first.
3. I exercise or get some walking in. This stops you from feeling sluggish.
4. The first time I think about taking a break, I tell myself to accomplish just one more thing before I do.

5. You have to mentally choose to push yourself forward by thinking about the outcome of achieving your goals vs. what it would be like to accomplish nothing.

When it's all said and done, it starts with pure discipline. If you aren't willing or have the fire inside to achieve in life, nothing can force you to. It comes from within. Success, positive momentum, and winning have to come from inside.

IF YOU COULD TEACH THE WORLD ONE THING BASED ON YOUR LIFE EXPERIENCES, WHAT WOULD IT BE?

I've been asked this question many times, and it really comes down to one thing. Just be authentic by being yourself. Too often, we are peppered by images in society of what is cool and trendy, and so many of us are constantly seeking approval of others to justify our own self-worth.

This is all just "wasted" energy. By focusing on a being an authentic person who brings positivity and goodness to those around them, you can really be a light that shines for others. When you invest countless time and energy into worrying and seeking to impress others, you lose what is most important, which is giving the world the "real" version of you.

When you are authentic, you have the ability to accomplish more, inspire others, and really live as yourself, not an image you think others want.

Believe in yourself and be yourself.

WHAT WAS THE MOST IMPORTANT LESSON YOU LEARNED FROM YOUR FATHER?

My father taught me so many things, but I'd have to say the biggest lesson I learned from him was the value of putting in the preparation work to succeed. Putting in the hard work that's required to set yourself up for success.

So many people want to achieve goals, have nice houses, cars, millions of dollars, etc. but are NOT willing to do the prep work to make their dreams happen.

See, my dad made me focus on the fundamentals of success, which is doing the work behind the scenes to prepare. Studying, practicing, working, and doing the things that nobody sees or thinks is glamorous. It's this work, though, when you have your opportunity to shine, you are ready to excel.

If you aren't willing to put in the work, don't expect to succeed.

WHAT IS THE SKILLSET OF A GOOD CEO?

To be a good CEO you have to have a variety of skills. Here are a few that quickly come to mind.

1. Ability to inspire and communicate the company vision. You have to have charisma and be able to get the entire company excited about the mission.
2. Have great people skills. Know how to relate to your staff and have great employee relations. Your people are what drives your success as a leader.
3. You have to be able to learn new concepts fast, and then make solid decisions based on the best information you have at the time.

4. Have the ability to make the tough decisions. A CEO has to make decisions that are in the best interests of the company.
5. You have to be a good delegator who delegates to a great support staff of leaders who can execute your vision.
6. Be an innovator. A CEO needs to breed a culture of innovation in which creativity and the best ideas are allowed to come forth.
7. A good general knowledge of all aspects of the business, which includes financials, sales, marketing, product, and technology.

IS 40 TOO OLD TO BECOME AN ENTREPRENEUR?

Not at all. Becoming an entrepreneur is not about your age but whether you have the drive and creativity to make it happen. When I graduated from college, I had no idea how to really start a business, so I ended up working in a cubicle at a dead-end job. I knew inside I wanted to be an entrepreneur, so I started testing the waters, starting side businesses in my free time. (Fitness training, selling real-estate, blogging, etc.)

I learned a ton, had some small successes, but never made it big. The key, though, was, I had the fire inside, kept learning, and kept trying.

It took me until I was 33 when I finally launched the successful company I lead today. Had I launched it when I was younger, I simply wouldn't have had the real world experience needed. Even now in my 40s, I keep learning every day.

I think an older entrepreneur can definitely succeed if they have the drive inside to make it happen. The fears I see are that many times, older potential entrepreneurs are more risk-averse and have more obligations than recent college graduates. This is totally understandable.

Here's my advice if you want to test the waters

Try a side business. (The benefit of this is that you get to try the entrepreneurial world in your free time.) Another good reason is that you'll likely be tired from your regular job, and finding time for your side business will test your ability to push on. In reality, becoming an entrepreneur will be much tougher than your day job. You have to find the energy, drive, and passion even when you're past the "fun" stage of starting a company.

HOW DO CEO'S WHO SLEEP FOR ONLY 4-5 HOURS DAILY MANAGE TO FUNCTION AND RUN MULTI-MILLION DOLLAR COMPANIES?

Take it from one that has bootstrapped and has led a multi-million dollar company for years, the reality of 4–5 hours of sleep is a lot of hype. Sure, I've spent time sleeping little during various phases of my company or when the need arises, but as an overall practice, sleeping 4–5 hours simply isn't healthy. As an entrepreneur/CEO, it often sounds "super-human" to tell people you sleep very little, and in fact, there might just be people who do that, but.... are they taking a short nap during the day? We don't know really.

If you look at it from the "entrepreneur" perspective, you work "24/7," so yes, you might sleep 4–5 hours some nights but sleep longer some days and even fit in naps. It becomes a way of life, so you sleep when you need to, but my advice would be to forget the nonsense. Don't try to emulate this 4–5 hours myth and focus on sleeping. You'll be better off and healthier.

WHAT IS THE REAL MEANING OF SUCCESS IN LIFE?

In my opinion, a successful life is one in which you have a positive impact on those around you and helps bring energy and light into their lives. Many of us get caught up in trying to impress everyone in a world that, too often, makes us all feel inferior.

If you focus on being a good person, be authentic and genuinely bring energy and enthusiasm to those around you, then you are on the right path.

The mission is to be a person who has helped better those around you, inspire people toward goodness and positivity to their lives. This leaves a legacy of success that others can look to and build on.

WHAT ARE THE MOST IMPORTANT SOFT SKILLS YOUR EMPLOYEES NEED?

1. **People skills.** For those who grew up in a digital world, this can be challenging, but you have to learn how to interact with other human beings—face to face. You need to know how to how to shake hands, make proper eye contact, and dress properly for the job. It's also important to erect social "boundaries" in the workplace. Don't "overshare" details of your personal life with colleagues and superiors. Most importantly, you must display empathy—to show that you actually care about others. Some people think it's okay to be rude on the job because "it's business; not personal." In reality, how you treat others couldn't be more personal.

2. **Communication skills.** You must know how to write and speak effectively in a business context. How you

communicate shapes how others perceive your intelligence and abilities. Proper spelling and grammar are essential, and so is a tone and style that's more formal than what people use in text messages. (Do *not* use texting abbreviations and jargon in business correspondence!) Just as critical: know how to listen—*really listen*—to your colleagues, bosses, and customers.

3. **Critical Thinking Skills.** The ability to use Google to search for data is a good start. But a more important skill is the ability to *interpret* the data and develop solutions. Bring *solutions* to your boss, not just explanations of the problems. General Patton once said, "Never tell people how to do things. Tell them what to do, and they will surprise you with their ingenuity." In other words, don't expect to be micro-managed. Most bosses are too busy to mentor or micro-manage junior employees. They expect results, not excuses, and expect that you'll figure out how to do the job on your own time.

HOW CAN YOU BECOME MORE CONFIDENT?

First off, confidence comes from having the internal knowledge that you have the skills and are prepared to give it your best to succeed.

In reality, though, many of us suffer from lack of confidence due to outside forces. We worry if people are judging us and that we don't measure up to what others expect.

People often place way too much importance on the opinion of others, but in reality, most people are not worried nor do they care what you are doing.

Our lack of confidence comes from "false" internal thoughts we create in our own head of what others are thinking about us.

So... how do you become confident? You start being yourself. You realize that your only goal should be the best "you" that you can be. You prepare yourself to succeed, you do the work required, you know that failure in some situations is likely, but you look at things with the mindset that each "failure" is simply feedback to help you do better on the next attempt.

Confidence builds over time, when you start to realize that "failures" are forgotten and you take the lessons as growth opportunities. If you can do this and become happy simply by being the "authentic" you, you will start to ignore the thoughts about impressing others. Once you can do that, you can really live and go out and try things without fear of being judged. That's when you begin to have confidence.

IS COLLEGE WORTH IT?

I went to college, got a degree, and I use very little from what I learned. I gained 10x more knowledge outside of college than I ever did in the classroom.

I come from a family of teachers. Dad, Uncle, Aunt, Grandmother... etc. and education was always emphasized, so I had an innate drive to soak up knowledge on my own.

So, is spending thousands and thousands of dollars, having huge student loans, and basically four years out of the fast moving job market worth it? It's a tough call.

If I know what I did today, I would have focused on becoming the entrepreneur I am today a lot sooner. It may or may not have accelerated my goals, but I would have been a lot happier. College is likely a good choice if you are going into a defined career where a degree is vital. If your career path doesn't, then the cost and time probably isn't.

I'd say, if you're not sure, take a break, try various things and be creative. Don't be in a rush. Too many young people feel a rush to follow a path that society and everyone defines. You have to ultimately do what you think will provide you the best route to achieve your dreams. If it means delaying college for a few years to find what you truly are passionate about, then so be it.

HOW CAN I OVERCOME MY FEAR OF PUBLIC SPEAKING?

I think the best way is to practice by doing short videos.

If you spend time recording yourself speaking about different topics and putting together short videos, you'll learn much more about how to speak.

With a cell phone, you can practice over and over and then watch yourself. Sure, you may stumble on your words, make mistakes, and not like the way you sound, but don't worry. Just keep at it.

Over time, you'll start to improve in your confidence and delivery. Add that to studying other quality speakers, and you'll be on your way.

Lastly, remember to just be authentic. Sure, you might talk too fast and not be polished, but nothing beats authenticity.

Once you have mastered talking in videos, you can move on to small groups. Just remember, most people don't speak in public, and most people don't pay attention anyway, so your preparation will have you far ahead of the curve.

HOW CAN I BECOME A MILLIONAIRE IN LESS THAN A YEAR?

The focus on becoming a millionaire in one year will likely ensure you won't. Not that I'm against achieving goals, but you have to put in the work, effort, and have a good product or service customers are willing to pay for.

To truly build a real legitimate business, you have to focus on perfecting your product or service and be able to effectively sell it. That's where all focus should be. The moment you start thinking only about money is when you take your eyes off the ball of what's key.... Building a real business.

As far as businesses to start with little money. Service-based businesses, social media management, or businesses that don't require costly product you need to have on hand would be your best bet.

In closing, just remember, focusing too much on becoming a millionaire fast without a realistic outlook dooms many to failure. Money is great, but focusing intently on building a long-term lasting business is a better long-term goal.

WHAT ARE THE MOST EFFECTIVE AND EFFICIENT WAYS TO USE SOCIAL MEDIA TO EXPAND YOUR BUSINESS?

The best way is to keep it simple, authentic, and targeted toward your core audience.

Remember, your target market/audience is where your number one focus should be. Where are they and what platform do they use?

Once you know your market you can focus in on delivering personalized, authentic content. You should add in video, your own content, write posts, and keep it active and fun. The rest will depend on whether you are b2b or b2c.

The more active and real you are, the better. Inactivity leads to obscurity.

HOW CAN I BECOME SUCCESSFUL?

First off, to be successful, you have to define what your idea of success is. Success for some is failure for others. Success needs to be defined.

I wanted to be an NBA basketball player when I was in high school, and that would have been my "success," but it didn't happen. I did, however, find success in business and entrepreneurship. You have to remember, success often comes after many failures and attempts.

Also, you have remember that achieving success in anything is hard work, but it's also a combination of so many other factors. No one can guarantee success even if you have all of the skills, do everything right, and plan perfectly.

All you can do and ask for is to "set yourself up" for success. That means you are ready when the opportunity presents itself to give it your best shot.

You have to do all of the preparation work that many people don't like to do even knowing the outcome is uncertain. It's often the unglamorous work that is behind the scenes and nobody sees. This can include learning new skills, practicing, studying, etc.

The biggest takeaway is that to be successful, you have to be willing to prepare, give it your best, and if you fail, don't let the failures weigh you down. They should serve as lessons for growth to help you become the eventual "success" you want to be.

WHAT IS THE BEST SOCIAL MEDIA TECHNIQUE FOR SMALL & MIDSIZE BUSINESSES

Your best bet is to pick one or two key social media platforms. Ideally, these should be the main social media avenues that your customers are most likely to frequent. (This is different if you are a B2B company vs. a B2C.)

Once you do that, focus on good content and personalize your company. Short videos, original content, micro-content, and valuable information can go a long way in getting your name out. The biggest problem for most businesses is obscurity. There is so much media and noise out there these days that it's hard to get noticed. This is why it's essential to be laser-focused on our target market as well.

In summary,

1. Pick one or two key platforms.
2. Personalize it with great content.
3. Target the right market and focus like a laser.
4. And lastly, you have to be consistent. Most fail in this area.

HOW CAN I BECOME CHARISMATIC?

The biggest keys to energizing people and being charismatic is to bring energy, enthusiasm, and authenticity.

It's that's simple. It's hard not to get excited about something when the person who is talking to you is upbeat, positive, and enthusiastic.

You can learn to become more charismatic by:

1. **Being yourself and being authentic.** By connecting with others, you create a genuine bond with people. Those who

put on a "fake" persona aren't real, and people can detect that. The best version of you is "YOU." Too often, people falsely think in their minds that they are inferior, and as a result, pretend to be what they think others want them to be. Don't fall into that trap. Be yourself.

2. **Bringing energy to everything you do.** You have to bring a buzz or excitement to what you are doing. Nothing is worse than a person with no energy. They sap the room full of life and bring everyone down. The quickest way to get people to rally around you is with energy.

3. **Lastly, enthusiasm.** This is similar to energy, but this is the confidence and forward-looking energy that truly gets everyone to want to join you on your mission. When you mesh energy, enthusiasm, and authenticity, you have the perfect formula for charisma.

HOW CAN I STOP WORRYING ABOUT WHAT OTHER PEOPLE THINK?

Most of our lives we are conditioned subconsciously and even overtly that if we aren't doing what everyone else is doing or we are different, then we're not cool enough or good enough.

Marketing, advertising, and pop culture feeds off of everyone's insecurities of not measuring up.

See, this creates a ton of pressure and feelings of inadequacy for so many people.

So how can you break free from this vicious cycle? You have to realize that life is short. What most people are thinking about is **NOT** you. **They are thinking about themselves.**

When you look at things from that perspective, it gives you a new way to if thinking.

For example, people fear speaking in front of large groups. I used to feel the same way. What are they thinking? Are the laughing at me? Are their smiles really smirks with them doubting everything I am saying?

Your mind can run on for days wondering what everyone is thinking. In reality, though, most people are thinking, " Thank goodness it's not me having to speak up there" or they are tuned out and daydreaming about their own life. Very few are actually even paying attention or listening.

When you understand that we, as people, naturally doubt ourselves and are thinking that exact same thing, it's actually empowering. You begin to say....."Hey, I'm actually doing something that others find difficult". It begins to strengthen you.

Over time, the more and more you go out and push your limits, you begin to become stronger, less fearful, and actually gain confidence to be yourself without concern of other's thoughts.

So, just remember, life is short, and all of these worries will never matter 10, 15, or 100 years from now. Also, don't forget there are around 7.8 Billion people in the world who don't even know who you are. They aren't thinking or focused on your "perceived" shortcomings.

Enjoy life, live strong, and become the best version of YOU that you can be!

WHICH IS MORE IMPORTANT FOR A CEO, LEADERSHIP SKILLS OR EXPERIENCE IN MULTIPLE AREAS?

Leadership by far is most important. See, you can learn sales, marketing, financials, etc. But nothing can beat a highly motivated, inspirational leader.

As the CEO, I believe you have to bring a high level of energy and enthusiasm into the job. Your mission is to be the visionary who can motivate the entire organization into driving toward success.

If the CEO is a dull, boring, paper pusher and has the "corporate" financial "suit" mold, you'll simply have yet another boring company. Yes, many CEOs fit that mold because investors and companies feel "safe" with boring.

For companies though, that truly want to become the best, a driven inspirational leader who connects with the employees and brings the message to everyone can deliver far better results in the long run.

So there's your answer. Leadership is key.

WHAT IS YOUR MOST POWERFUL TIP?

After everything I've learned, the most powerful tip any of us should focus on is just being an authentic person. Be yourself.

Society today makes so many people feel inferior. We are made to believe we aren't good enough. We're constantly being judged, compared, compartmentalized, and labeled.

The best thing anyone can do is just be a good authentic person and forget about trying to impress others and be someone who you think others will like.

If you focus on being the best "You" you can be, you can achieve great things and be a shining light to others.

WHY IS THERE SUCH A FASCINATION WITH BECOMING AN ENTREPRENEUR?

In the past, young people wanted to be pro athletes, actors, singers, and movie stars, because media was limited, and so were opportunities. If you wanted to be a star in the past, you had to follow traditional routes, but today, it's all changed. You still had entrepreneurs in past, but I think technology has leveled the playing field and has provided so many opportunities to build businesses that couldn't have been built in the past. Look at the YouTubers, many are more famous with young people than athletes.

Technology has opened up so many new avenues for creativity and entrepreneurship.

Entrepreneurship is now seen as more exciting and glamorous partly because of the stories of Unicorn startups worth billions, and also the ability for people to bypass the "gatekeepers" and start their own companies with little money. Publishing, video production, video games, virtual businesses, all which were limited years ago.

All of this gives a young person a sense of excitement knowing they can make it on their own instead of following the route we were all sold years ago; that you simply go to college, get a degree, and work in a cubicle for someone else.

The reality of becoming a successful entrepreneur is hard, but it serves as something many people can aspire to. It can also be a path to freedom for those who get it right.

WHAT ARE SOME OF THE BIGGEST RED FLAGS IN AN INTERVIEW?

Over the years I have interviewed many candidates from entry-level to executive roles. For me, the biggest red flag is if a candidate relies heavily on (and touts) their college degree or MBA as the reason they are best qualified for the job.

Some candidates are so enamored with their book knowledge and degree that they feel this makes them an "expert" in business or how to run a company.

This, in my opinion, is a sure sign of a weak candidate, as in reality, a piece of paper has no value. It's how a person uses their education and applies it to their overall career.

I focus more on a person's energy, enthusiasm, willingness to be a team player, and desire to learn within our company. Simply coming in with arrogance by having a diploma from a certain university doesn't impress me.

So my tip is this... if you interview a candidate and they possess a sense of entitlement due to their education, you might want to think twice.

LIFE: WHAT ONE PIECE OF ADVICE WOULD YOU GIVE TO YOUR YOUNGER SELF?

Don't waste your time worrying about what others might be thinking or saying about you.

Most people, in reality, are focused on themselves anyway and don't care. Often, in our minds, we "think" or imagine that others are criticizing us or we aren't measuring up to some perceived fake "standard."

It can cause you to waste a TON of unnecessary energy and time on things that have no relevance to your life or dreams.

Just go out and focus on becoming the best YOU that you can be, and ignore the "haters" and people who try to push you off your path.

Stay focused, be positive, and remember, most things are just noise and are irrelevant.

IS AN MBA DEGREE NECESSARY FOR SUCCESS IN BUSINESS?

It sounds like an oxymoron, but most people I have met with a Masters in Business (MBA) are actually the least skilled, knowledgeable, or qualified to run a business, yet are some of the most arrogant and entitled acting people I know.

Too many people place their hopes and dreams on a piece of paper but fail to understand that business success is more than a degree. It's about the intangibles, such as drive, hard work, perseverance, communication skills, problem-solving, ability to learn concepts on your own, and the ability to lead a team.

Now don't get me wrong, I think education is great. I have a university degree, too, but if you are looking for what it takes to be a success in business, an MBA is only a "tool." It's merely education and book knowledge. An MBA can be valuable for the right person who seeks to use that knowledge to better themselves. An MBA as a vital part of success in business?.... eh... No.

If you want to get an MBA to better your knowledge, sure, go ahead. It could cost easily 100k to 200k with no guarantee of a return. The reality is that most entrepreneurs I know are more focused on building a company and going after their dreams vs. a framed piece of paper on a wall.

WHAT IS THE TOUGHEST DECISION YOU EVER MADE AS A START-UP BUSINESS OWNER?

The toughest decision I had to make during our start-up phase was firing a client who brought in over half of our revenue when we were just trying to get our momentum going as a company.

One of the hardest things a business owner will encounter when starting up a company is getting clients. If you don't have paying customers, you don't have a business.

Unfortunately, in many industries, the first clients you get will be some of the most difficult because the established and proven competitors of yours already know they are difficult and don't want their business. So, you are left with the really tough ones.

I had to make the decision to part ways with a really difficult customer knowing it would put pressure on us financially, but here's why it makes sense.

If you spend 80% of your time dealing with one difficult customer, you are neglecting your truly valuable customers and ALL of the potential market you can be going after to really grow your business.

It's the philosophy of taking one step back to be able to jump 2, 3, or 10 steps forward! And guess what? It worked!

HOW DOES ONE ANALYZE A BUSINESS?

I think you have to analyze a business similar to how Marcus Lemonis does on his show "The Profit." I think it's a good, fun show to watch, and it gives the average person a little insight on how to view a business.

You do have to look at the **People, Product, and Process.**

You also have to know your numbers and how to analyze a profit and loss statement as well as a balance sheet.

To me, personally, If I'm looking at a company, I need to know if the top people are good leaders, are they highly motivated and do they think "company" first? You can't have "what's in it for me" people in your company. Also, are the staff excited about their job and do they buy into the mission?

Next, is the product or service good and is there a viable market for it? If it's a good product and there's a true market for it, then that is a huge key.

Lastly, how is the business running? Are operations efficient or are there areas that drive up costs. Are there too many manual processes? If the operations and process are good, then the company is on the right track.

Once you assess those factors, you have to look at the books.

Is the company profitable? Is there debt, and if so, how much? Is the company growing, flat, or declining? These are all factors you have to look at.

WHAT ADVICE CAN YOU GIVE A FIRST-TIME MANAGER?

My advice is to not let the power go to your head. That's the first way to have an angry team below you. When I was working for an insurance company during my first few years out of college, the insurer I was working for promoted several young, and I must say "unqualified," people into team leader and management positions. The first thing they did was go from being nice as co-workers to being transformed into monsters.

They let their perceived "power" go to their heads and treated everyone around them as though we were all their serfs.

Here's the deal. To effectively lead, it's not about being rude, aggressive, and bossy. It's about leading from the front and demonstrating the way things should be done by example. You may need to be firm eventually, but you have to first explain to everyone what the mission is and what you expect. You also need to be a teacher and help guide your team as a manager not simply bark out orders.

So for any of you who are new to a managerial position, just remember to treat people as you would want to be treated and truly look to grow your skills. Nobody knows it all, and it's a learning experience. Kindness and teamwork go a lot further than trying to act like a tyrant.

That's my two cents.

WHY DO YOU TREAT THE CEO THE SAME AS THE JANITOR?

You can conversely state... you should treat the Janitor the same as the CEO.

As a CEO, I don't see myself as a CEO. I am a person. I have worked many jobs in life, such as cleaning bathrooms in McDonald's, maintenance jobs, and even had a cubicle one as well.

Everyone should be treated with respect, and every job has value and every person has value.

The position in a job doesn't make anyone better than others. It's just a title.

When it comes to treating people a certain way, just focus on being a nice person, respect others, and do the right thing.

WHAT SINGLE TRAIT CAN A PERSON HAVE TO BE A SUCCESSFUL ENTREPRENEUR?

Most businesses fail. Becoming a successful entrepreneur is extremely hard, and you will encounter some of the most stressful times in your life.

There will be times where you won't sleep at night, you won't know if you can pay your staff or even yourself. You will have to face so many different things at one time and still be able to keep it all together and keep moving forward.

You can have the best product, service, or software but if you don't have the ability to keep coming back and pushing ahead through adversity, you won't make it.

Thus... **perseverance**

DOES A CEO REALLY WORK 15 HOURS A DAY?

When you are a CEO or business owner/entrepreneur, there is no work day in my opinion. There's no 9–5 job. Having bootstrapped and built a company from the ground up into a national company, which I am the CEO of, you simply work as much as you have to, which is a lot.

I often start my day at 6:30 or 7am and don't finish doing some type of work-related activity until 8pm. I still go for a 45-minute walk every day, I lift weights, have dinner with my family, and take time to rest.

The reality is nobody is going to sit at a desk for 15 straight hours.

It goes back to a mindset. Most CEO/business owners/entrepreneurs simply work to get the job done. For me, it's a lifestyle. I enjoy it and don't see it as work.

As a CEO, there are so many responsibilities to keep the company moving ahead, from marketing, sales, finance, strategy, HR, product, etc. that you have to carve out time to focus on current activity in each department, and it's done throughout the day.

There are days I may be in meetings, literally, all day, while some days, I have no meetings. It varies, so there is always something I have to be working on.

The reality is I have to know when to stop and actually pull myself away from work.

WHAT IS THE SINGLE MOST UNDERRATED TRAIT A PERSON CAN HAVE?

Optimism

We live in a world where every news cycle is negative, and people are seemingly inundated with negativity around every corner. It's easy to fall into a trap where everything seems to be headed down the tubes, but if you take a step back, and remember that each and every one of us has the ability to inject positivity into the world.

I think people who operate from optimism are out there looking to find a brighter future and spread a positive mind-set. Tune out the negativity and look to find the good things in life. Build strong networks of positive, like-minded people, and do good.

If more people took this outlook and worked on this trait, you'd see massive change.

HOW MANY BOOKS DOES A CEO READ IN A YEAR?

I can't speak for other CEOs but I personally read 6 books and listened to 12 audio versions of books. So, basically, 18 books for the year.

I listen to the audio versions when traveling or when I'm on the move, walking, or driving. I am a huge believer in gaining as much knowledge as possible in many diverse areas.

I read books on science, ancient civilizations, philosophy, health, business, etc. It's always good to keep your mind active and growing.

WHO DO YOU ADMIRE IN BUSINESS?

I admire many but idolize none. Here's why. Everyone is human, and even the most famous success stories have faults in so many areas. The best way to look at things is to focus on learning the best you can from everyone, and ultimately, build your own unique formula for success.

Don't get caught up in hero worship. Learn everything you can, and build a formula that others may admire someday.

HOW CAN A NICE PERSON LEARN TO BE A LEADER?

A nice person can learn to become a solid leader by reading and studying other successful leaders. I have read countless books from the top business people out there over the years and glean nuggets of wisdom from everyone to create my own style. There are also various courses you can take, which can also help. Leadership growth and learning is a continual process, and you never know it all.

Being a "nice" person shouldn't hold you back from being an effective leader.

Entrepreneur's Field Manual

You have to realize that leadership isn't about being a rude or mean person in the first place. Unfortunately, throughout my career in the working world, I've witnessed good employees turn from nice "workers" into tyrants the moment they were given some semblance of power. Why? Because they didn't know how to truly lead and were never given proper guidance.

See, a naive person thinks that leadership is about barking out orders, commanding people, and "taking charge" to show everyone who's the boss.

As a leader, you do have to be firm and possess the ability to "command," but it can be done in a way that inspires everyone. The one pitfall of being "too" nice, though, is that your team and employees can run amok if there is no "command presence" from the leader. You can be strong without getting run over.

All of this can be taught to a degree. A leader can be nice and still get results through teamwork, an inspiring vision, and getting into the trenches with the team and leading from the front. To me, leadership is a combination of all of these attributes. You have to embody leadership. It's not sitting back and just commanding. It's about becoming an active participant in the process.

WHAT ARE THE BIGGEST LESSONS YOU HAVE LEARNED IN THE CORPORATE WORLD BEFORE YOU STARTED YOUR OWN BUSINESS?

I'm a very positive and enthusiastic person, but as an entrepreneur at heart, my personal distaste for the corporate world I experienced was the inspiration for me to take the entrepreneurial leap.

The corporate world can be a rough place, and for those with no experience, it can be an eye-opener.

After graduating from college and having absolutely zero real-world business experience, I came in at the bottom. Oh, did I have a lot to learn.

1. **The most qualified people aren't always in charge.** That's right, people in many of the lower and middle management positions were simply unqualified and poor leaders. Most of their day was spent in maintaining their position and ensuring nobody outshined them. This often led to low morale.

2. **Office politics are real.** Following #1, this goes hand in hand. The lure of future promotions and the fight to gain the attention of senior executive leadership often created a tense environment where teamwork was rare and employees were looking to step on others to move up.

3. **The best ideas were often ignored.** Those with creative ideas who brought them to management often had them stolen and repackaged by the supervisors. Creativity and trying new approaches were generally ignored leaving the company stagnant.

4. **Entrepreneurs don't flourish.** If you have the mindset of an entrepreneur who is wanting to drive forward change, bring creativity and innovation, and move fast, the corporate world wasn't the place. It was the spark that inspired me to take the leap and strike out on my own.

So what did I learn during my corporate years? I learned how to build a dynamic company that would be the opposite of what I experienced. I would build the company where I wished I had worked. The lessons I learned on how NOT to run a company have enabled me to build a leading firm, while at the same time, give employees a chance to excel where I didn't in the corporate world.

WHY DO SO MANY STARTUPS FAIL?

The reason so many startups fail is a combination of factors, but here are four that come to mind.

1. **Is there even a market for the product or service?** Today, you see so many startups in areas that make no sense. Do I really need an app for this or that? Some of the ideas out there are so silly and worthless, yet people are trying to build a business in areas where this is no market. I like to joke about ideas... maybe I should start an "on demand" mobile app service that can take out my trash for me or pick up after my dog. I mean, to some degree, that's where the level of some "start ups' have gone. There is a point where some "innovation" is not innovation but simply ideas thrown against a wall hoping something will stick.

2. **The leadership and founders don't have the fire.** Yep, that's right. Many startups who receive cash infusions from investors don't have true respect for money when it's not theirs. They don't have real skin in the game, so if the startup fails... Oh well, it will look good on a resume that you were part of a "startup" that tried, pivoted, or

exited. At least you "failed fast." Personally, I don't have much respect for that type of entrepreneur. As one who bootstrapped to success, I see it through a different lens. One where your own money, credit, house, and everything is on the line. When you have that kind of motivation, you persevere, you bring all you have to make it work. Even then, there is no guarantee of success, but at least you're fully committed.

3. **Don't have the competitive drive.** As one who comes from an athletic background and years in competitive sports, I see business as the ultimate sport. Those who lead a startup that don't have the competitive fire to go after the market and compete will fail. Not everyone has that ability to think with that mindset. If you're not working hard and putting in the true effort, someone else is, and they will beat you when it's game time. If the top-down leadership is not obsessed about beating out the competition and delivering a great product or service to their customers, then who will be? That's right, your competitors.

4. **The team members aren't fully committed.** Yes, it does come down to having a team that can make it happen. Everyone is "excited" during the launch of a company, but do the team members have the ability to work together for the common goal? Unfortunately, people's priorities change, some don't have the fire to keep at it, and when you have infighting, this can lead to a disaster. It's simple.... if there's no driving force or individual that keeps the eyes and mission on the goal of doing what's best for the

company vs. what's best for the individual, then you can expect an implosion.

There are countless other reasons and ways a startup can fail, and no idea is a sure winner, but the mission for any startup should be to set themselves up for success by doing everything possible to be in the best position to succeed.

HOW DO YOU OVERCOME THE FEAR OF ENTREPRENEURIAL FAILURE?

Let's start with reality. Most businesses fail. So if you are thinking about taking the entrepreneurial leap, you have to accept that the odds are stacked against you.

I tried many things before I built the successful company I run today. I tried real estate (hated it), helped my brother with one of the first online music magazines in the 1990s (didn't know how to monetize it), and tried online fitness coaching (again, couldn't monetize it). So I encountered my own set of "failures," but it was through these so-called "failures" that I gained so much knowledge that helped build the business person I am today.

See, you can't have a fear of failure. All you can do is set yourself up for success by doing all the right things you can in hopes of stacking the odds in your favor.

Now.... another important thing. It's mindset. True winners, and those who succeed, don't see "failures" as even failures. You have to have a selective type of memory that categorizes them as just minor speed bumps on the way to your ultimate success. You learn the lesson, you grow and you move on. Nobody is sitting around focused on your perceived failures, so why should you.

Life is short, and why waste time being fearful of taking a leap and going after your dreams? You'll feel much worse if you don't go after them.

DOES YOUR MOTIVATION COME FROM WANTING TO SUCCEED OR AVOIDING FAILURE?

For me, personally, I am motivated by wanting to succeed and become the best I can be. Nobody "wants" to fail at anything in life, but the reality is you aren't going to succeed at everything, so you have to accept there will be "failures" and minor setbacks. That in no way means you have to take failures with an "oh well" attitude. You just can't dwell on the negative and squelch your motivation to succeed.

I believe when you are motivated by wanting to succeed and strive for greatness, you are doing it because you're passionate about it and want to achieve vs. being motivated by fear of failure. What drives me every day is the simple motivation of getting better, doing better, and being the best person I can be in all facets. I want to keep improving.

If you learn to enjoy and embrace the "process" of driving forward to succeed, this is where true growth happens. With this mindset, success or failure is never a finality, it's a process of growth.

Others may have a different view, but that's just my thoughts.

WHAT CAN I LEARN/KNOW RIGHT NOW IN 10 MINUTES THAT WILL BE USEFUL FOR THE REST OF MY LIFE?

Eliminate worry.

In my opinion, this can go a long way to a better life.

Most things that we all worry about have no value. We invest so much time, effort, and energy into worrying about things that either never happen or have no place taking up any of our mental energy.

And guess what, wasted mental energy on worry can make you tired, sleep poorly, and create a cascade of other negative effects that are not good for your health.

By simply learning to be ruthless in eliminating needless worry and wandering thoughts of negativity, you can see dramatic results in your life.

We are all human, and achieving this is extremely hard, but if one tries to make a conscious effort to minimize worry and needless anxiety, you will at least be headed in the right direction.

In the society we live in that's bombarded with negativity seemingly everywhere in the news, social media, etc., it can be hard to escape.

I think, though, that any effort to eliminate the negativity and worry can move the needle toward a better life, success, and happiness.

That's my two cents.

HOW CAN I BE SURE PEOPLE WON'T STEAL MY IDEA DURING A PITCH?

Let's be realistic. Most people have an overinflated view of their ideas and how innovative they are.

There are rarely any ideas that are so game-changing that someone else can't tweak in some way and compete with you in the market. My advice is to think less about people stealing your idea and more about how you will actually make it become a reality.

Everyone talks about ideas. Heck, I hear ideas all the time from people. People can dream up so many things at parties, at the coffee shop, and with their friends, but a very, very, very few can actually take an idea, flesh it out, and make it happen.

Also, not to sound negative, but most people don't care about your idea. The most difficult thing in business is overcoming obscurity. If you're unknown, you can talk and scream out the BEST idea in the world and the likelihood of anyone actually paying attention is slim to none. The hardest part is to get someone to actually listen to you and believe your idea is any good.

During a pitch, an investor wants to know if there is a market, how big it is, how does your product or solution make a difference, and can it or does it make money? Most importantly, they want to know if the leadership team is any good and can they execute.

So, my advice would be to not worry about the cloak and dagger games of your top-secret idea, and focus like a laser on the execution of it.

WHAT IS THE SINGLE MOST EFFECTIVE PIECE OF FINANCIAL ADVICE YOU'VE EVER RECEIVED?

I remember at a young age, my parents told me... "You don't spend money you don't have."

The biggest issue many people have is personal debt and lack of sufficient income to ever climb out of it.

Now, I'm a big believer in finding ways to grow your income. That's a great way to achieve your financial dreams and create security for you and your family. Higher income can also help you correct some past spending mistakes as you can afford to pay down debt faster if you don't keep spending. Unfortunately, though, many people are unable to really go after their dreams because they've put themselves in such a bind having no money, a mountain of debt, and insufficient income.

From a very young age, through college and when I entered the working world, I adhered to the philosophy of "don't buy what you can't afford." That means I lived well below my means to maintain great credit and build for my future. Others around me were buying nice cars, spending money like crazy, and mortgaging their future. Did I feel jealous at the time? At times, yes.

In hindsight, though, simply adhering to my philosophy allowed me to build a solid future without the stress of debt.

DO INTERESTED VCS LIKE SHORT PITCH DECKS OR DETAILED ONES?

First off, I bootstrapped my company from nothing into a very successful company without one penny of outside investment.

That's how the real world works for most true entrepreneurs. They grind it out.

Now.... over the years as we've built our company into a profitable, successful national company, I started to get the calls. Yes, I mean calls. Tons. Junior associates at VC and equity firms wanting to talk. Eventually, over time, we had the partners of these firms coming to meet us at our office.

So, my experience comes from already having built a successful business. Not going out with just an idea and pitching.... but from my perspective, having done over 100 of these "Pitches," it's all the same.

VC's and investors want concise and to the point decks that get to the meat of your idea, the market for it, who you are, and how you are going to make money.

They don't care about all of your app's bells and whistles, all the widgets and things you might think are cool. They want to know the solution you have works and does what you say. If you do a deep dive into all the tech talk, their eyes will glaze over.

They see so many pitches, they want to know in just a few minutes if your idea makes sense. It's about being to the point, what is your path to making money and gaining market share.

Just remember to be yourself as investors invest in people first. Bring energy, passion, and a great story with a path to success, and you will be on your way to doing well. Don't over think it.

WHAT ARE SOME THINGS THAT EVERY ENTREPRENEUR SHOULD KNOW BUT THAT NOBODY TEACHES WHEN STARTING THEIR FIRST BUSINESS?

1. **How to manage people.** One of the most challenging aspects of starting a company is building a cohesive team and keeping everyone inspired and focused on the company mission. You can have a great idea and product all day long, but if your people don't embody your vision, the company won't succeed.

2. **Choose your business partners wisely.** A bad business partner has the potential to be a royal headache who can suck morale away from the others. Everyone is happy during the start-up phase, but the relationship can sour over time as with anything in life.

3. **Understand that the team you start with won't necessarily be the right team you need years down the road.** Often, you outgrow the skillset of many of the original team members. It's hard to deal with, but to grow your company, you have to move past them and hire better and more qualified teammates.

4. **Firing people is not fun.** Nobody likes to tell people they don't cut it because it's tough and painful, but often, it's either them or the health of your company. As an entrepreneur, you have to always do what's best for your company.

HOW CAN A PERSON FIND THEIR GIFT/TALENT?

You have to get out and try as many things that interest you as possible and see if there is something that you are really good at. When you truly find what you love doing, it won't feel like work.

We all have interests and passions, but too often, we get stuck in adhering to societal norms. We end up listening to others (family, friends, etc.) who talk us down from our goals. They often encourage the "safe" route to a regular average job.

From my vantage point, I fell into the trap too for about 8 years until I decided to take the entrepreneurial leap. It just didn't sit right with me doing something I hated.

A lot of us go to college, study a field you don't have a true interest in, then get a job you're not passionate about. You might end up with a mountain of debt and regrets that you aren't doing what you love. If you take a step back and relax and really think, it's very likely you can think of things that interest you and you are good at. You just need to think outside of the traditional "9-5" job/career.

Once you find your strengths and talent... go all in!

You then need to focus on becoming the best you can be in that field. If it's truly your passion, it won't feel like work because you'll finally be doing something you love.

To get started you have to try many things, and don't be afraid to. Your life is yours, don't spend it living someone else's.

WHAT MOTIVATES YOU?

I wake up every day motivated to be the best I can be. Sure, that might sound cheesy, but what drives me are a few things;

1. I have a driven personality that likes to compete, I have a bit of a chip on my shoulder to prove myself in business, and I enjoy building a company from the ground up.
2. I'm motivated to create a great life for my family and also teach my kids how to be successful so they have a good role model. By leading by example, they learn the values and traits to forge their own success. It inspires me everyday to inspire them.
3. I'm motivated for all of my employees and the company I've built. I have a huge responsibility to make my organization a place where they can continue to grow their careers, provide stability, and better their skills.

To me, it's an internal drive to reach my potential, and at the same time, lift others up around me.

WHAT DOES A CEO DO?

The CEO is the person who runs the company. The buck stops with them.

With that title, though, comes immense responsibility. I am speaking from the mindset of a bootstrap entrepreneur who built a company from the ground up with not a penny of outside investment.

I take my job seriously, and ultimately, most major decisions end up coming from me.

So what does a CEO do from my perspective? Here are just a few off the top of my head.

1. You have to motivate and inspire your entire company and get everyone to buy into the vision. You are the inspirational leader.
2. You have to create a great strategy, know the marketplace, and keep your company competitive.
3. You are the face of the company, and you need to create the culture that defines your mission. Positive, forward thinking, and driven.
4. Be ready to take risks and make countless decisions in various areas of the company with the input of department executives.
5. You need to make sure there is money in the bank, spend wisely, and ensure you keep the company on a strong footing.
6. Accept responsibility and ownership that you are the one guiding the ship and do the best of your ability at all times, make every decision in the best interests of the company, and do the right thing.

WHAT IS YOUR BIGGEST OBSTACLE TO STAYING FOCUSED?

The biggest obstacle in today's world for everyone to stay focused is the constant buzz of news, information, entertainment, and social media.

There is so much going on at every moment that it can create a sense that you are "missing" out if you aren't dialed in 100% of the time.

All social media platforms, to some degree, are playing to our dopamine response with likes, new stories you don't want to miss, etc.

The key to break away and regain focus is to simply set aside time where you unplug.

Get outside and away from the electronic leash, use paper and a pen to write down thoughts, and do something that's away from "the digital world."

Focus requires extreme concentration and the ability to keep at something without distractions. When you free your mind from the nagging buzz of constant information, you set your self up for much better productivity. I, too, have to overcome this daily, and you have to consciously make the decision to reclaim your time.

HOW HARD IS IT TO BE AN ENTREPRENEUR?

It's extremely hard.

If you knew the truth of how hard it is, you'd probably run away fast as you can.

What?!! Why would a guy like me say such a thing?

Well, today we live in a world where many feel entitled to success without having to do much of anything. I see far too many people that "feel" they deserve to run a company, have a business, and enjoy the trappings of this "entrepreneur" lifestyle but don't want to do the hard work it takes.

Some people think that building company is as easy as coming up with ny idea, getting some venture money, wearing a hoodie, having a keg on tap in the office, enjoying some coffee shop meetings with their "successful" friends, running the company like a fraternity, and acting like you've made it.

That's not reality.

Hey, if you are willing to get real and get serious about being a success, then I can give it to you straight. Most businesses fail, and most entrepreneurs out there aren't even really entrepreneurs. They are fakers.

Here's what success really looks like from someone who has ground it out and didn't have investment money just handed to them.

- You're going to feel scared.
- You're going to doubt yourself.
- You're going to wonder how you will be able to pay your staff.
- You'll wonder if you'll have the money to make it to the next month.
- You'll be up late at night wondering what else can you do to move your company ahead.
- You'll worry if you can keep your clients.
- You'll wonder why new clients aren't knocking your doors down for your great product.
- You'll wonder if you'll even make it.
- You'll have friends and family doubt you.

WHAT ARE THE MOST COMMON MISTAKES FIRST TIME ENTREPRENEURS MAKE?
The list would be exhaustive, but I'll narrow it down to 4.

1. **Take any and every customer you can just to get business.** I know it's a double edge sword, but you can't bring on clients that suck away all of your time at the expense

of finding the "good," high-value customers that will allow you to grow and build your business.

2. **Feel like a loser because you haven't raised money.** There is "hype" about the companies that go out and raise capital, but that doesn't mean they are successful. You can bootstrap and build your company on your own and achieve much more. Don't fall into the "raise money" trap unless you truly need to do it and it really makes sense.

3. **Not managing money well.** Running a company and building something to last takes work. Just calling yourself an entrepreneur doesn't mean that's a license to live the high life and spend money like you've made it. Too often, people embrace the title "entrepreneur" but don't have the slightest idea how to run a company or manage their financials. They blow through money and the company flames out.

4. **Underestimating the sacrifices you will have to make to be successful.** I always say, "There is no guarantee of success, but you can at least do the work to set yourself up for success." In my opinion, there are countless people out there who want the title "entrepreneur" but are unwilling to do the work and grind it takes to truly build a company. If you want to make it, you have to commit. It's extremely hard and will consume nearly all of your time.

WHAT DO YOU THINK IS THE MOST IMPORTANT SKILL FOR A COMPANY TO FOCUS ON TO ENSURE SUCCESS?

It all comes down to one thing for the success of a company, and it's **customer service.**

You can have the best product, but if you have horrible customer, service you will turn clients away so fast it will make your head spin.

I think one of the most undervalued yet vital keys to a company is the emphasis on great customer interactions.

Every interaction with a customer or client is either an opportunity to amaze them or leave them dissatisfied.

The simple things such as empathy, enthusiasm, upbeat energy, listening to customer needs, and a true sense of wanting to help make a difference. It can go a LONG way to growing your business and creating a great reputation for your company.

So, my advice is simple. It doesn't matter what business you are in. Customer service and a genuine caring for the customer make a huge difference to failure or success.

WHAT ARE SOME TOP CEO SKILLS?

In my opinion, the CEO has to be the inspirational and defining leader of the company. They have to embody what the core of the company is and bring the vision to life. Here are 6 things that you have to be able to do.

1. **Inspirational.** You have to motivate and inspire your entire company and get everyone to buy into the vision. You are the inspirational leader.

2. **Be a strategist.** You have to create a great strategy, know the marketplace and keep your company competitive.

3. **Ability to create the culture.** You are the face of the company, and you need to create the culture that defines your mission. Positive, forward thinking, and driven.

4. **Be a decision maker.** Be ready to take risks and make countless decisions in various areas of the company with the input of department executives.

5. **Money skills.** You need to make sure there is money in the bank, spend wisely, and ensure you keep the company on a strong footing.

6. **Leadership.** Accept responsibility and ownership that you are the one guiding the ship, and do the best of your ability at all times, make every decision in the best interests of the company, and do the right thing.

HOW CAN I STOP FEARING FAILURE?

Too many people are stuck and stagnant because they live their lives worrying what others might think of them if they try something and fail.

Who cares.

Failure isn't permanent. It's a learning process.

I was a basketball player. If I miss a shot (a failure), I don't stop shooting. I keep shooting until I get into the groove and start making shots.

I'm a believer that you have to take positive action in the direction you want to go. Will it work out every time successfully? No. However, if you keep moving in a positive direction, you will get those little "victories," those little successes that add up.

If you are scared of failure, you have to ask yourself, why do you care? If you are worried about others judging you and making fun of you, just remember, those who do that are the ones who are insecure.

The easiest way to take positive action and break out of a rut of not taking action is simply doing an easy or small task that is just out of your comfort zone and get that little "win." Build on your small successes. You might even fail small but that's okay. Just keep taking small positive steps and tally up more "wins." After you gain some confidence, then try some bigger challenges.

Just remember, most people aren't focused on your failures. They are more worried about their own.

Life is short, so go after your dreams and become the best YOU that you can be.

WHY DO MOST ENTREPRENEURS COME ACROSS AS WANNABES?

Because a lot of them are.

We are living in the time of the biggest group of fake "entrepreneurs" in history.

In the past, an entrepreneur had to actually build a real company and make real money. They actually had to do the hard work, grind away, and dig deep. Today, most wannabes run when the hard work begins.

Today, everyone wants to claim the title of "entrepreneur" and tout the multiple businesses they started, money they raised, and talk a big game, all without actually making money.

The reality is most of their "entrepreneurial" talk happens at coffee shops with their buddies all living vicariously through maybe one or two successful friends. Heck, I know people like that. They talk the game, drop some "intellectual" vocabulary they learned in college, but have absolutely ZERO knowledge of what it takes to run a real company.

The fact that we see Unicorn stories of startups gaining HUGE valuations with no revenue while burning through cash gives pretty much anyone the license to call themselves "entrepreneur."

All you have to do is take the title, you never have to turn a profit. You can just try different things, and suddenly, you can call yourself a "serial entrepreneur." The next step is they eventually call themselves investors. All a bunch of BS.

In my book, you are NOT an entrepreneur unless you have built and grown at least one profitable, successful business. Anything else is fake.

DOES VC MONEY MAKE A STARTUP SUCCESSFUL?

If you buy into the hype, sure, it can make a company "appear" successful. If you are talking about making a company a profitable and successful one. No.

In business, money from a VC doesn't guarantee success. The market and your product will determine your ultimate success.

I think it's comical when I see companies who bleed money and burn through cash from investors only to raise yet another round. It's followed by a press release, and then some "industry" magazines that jump in an do stories on the company, and they get favorable press, yet.... No profitability.

I see these startups as lazy. They usually have the fancy office, perks, and hype without ever having put in the real work.

To me, the real entrepreneur that creates a successful startup is the one who grinds it out.

WHAT ARE THE THINGS THAT KEEP ENTREPRENEURS AND START-UP FOUNDERS AWAKE LATE AT NIGHT?

If you are going to take the entrepreneurial leap, you have to be able to handle stress. This is not the 9–5 world. It's 24/7/365. You live it, and unfortunately, there are times you going to be awake at night thinking.

So here are some things I've thought about back in the start-up days:

- Will I be able to make payroll for my staff (I can't even pay myself yet)?
- Will we have enough money in the bank to make it another month?
- My customers are 90 days late in paying. Will we ever get our money?
- Am I forgetting something I should be working on to move forward?
- What can I do to drive more sales?
- Will we even make it?
- What will I do if I can't make my house payment?
- How much do we have to buy food with?

- Why aren't clients knocking down our doors? We have the best product out there.
- Why do my friends and family doubt me?
- How can we market better to get more recognition?
- Why are staff so hard to manage? What can I do better?
- Will the bank renew our credit line?

Okay, you get the point.

As an entrepreneur, you pretty much worry about everything, and you know why? There is no safety net. Especially, if you are the one with your own personal money on the line.

You are on your own.

Now I'm talking about the true, bootstrap entrepreneur, not the VC funded startups where the founders have no skin in the game.

When it's your own home and personal assets pledged against a credit line, office space, and more, you have everything to lose. That's when you're going to be up late at night worrying.

But you know what? I might worry a bit, but I make sure I outworked my worry by getting up and doing things to drive the company ahead. There's always something I could be doing to gain just one bit of an advantage over the competitors. While they sleep, I work.

WHAT IS THE SECRET TO SUCCESS?

Most people don't realize the difference between success and failure is very tiny. Simply by changing one's attitude, working smart, and giving a solid effort, one can achieve amazing results that, otherwise, would seem impossible.

Here are seven key tips that can tilt the balance in your favor.

1. **Focus on continuous improvement.** Winners are always looking to find ways to improve their skills and knowledge. The opportunity to keep growing and learning is a lifelong process. You can always get better!

2. **Never be satisfied with temporary accomplishments.** The moment you think you've made it is the moment you've failed. Why? Complacency sets in, and you lose the fire inside. Success is only temporary, and you can never take it for granted.

3. **Look to lift up those around you.** Winners know that teamwork helps achieve big goals. Success happens when you elevate everyone around you. You can't do it alone.

4. **Don't blame others.** Those who focus on making excuses create negativity. Instead of thinking that everyone else is holding you back, focus on what you can do to move ahead and better yourself.

5. **Don't waste time.** Winners don't waste valuable time doing frivolous things that take focus away from their goals. While others party, watch TV, and play video games, winners are pushing ahead on their mission to succeed.

6. **Love the process.** You have to enjoy the process of achieving the small victories and working to become successful. It

will often take more time than you realize, but you have to relish the hard work and the climb.

7. **Don't quit.** Many people have amazing talents and skills they don't even realize exist. They fail because they never even try or they quit too soon. Learning to overcome challenges and perseverence is often the difference between reaching your goals or falling short.

WHY DOES IT SEEM LIKE THE ONLY GOAL FOR SOME ENTREPRENEURS IS TO GET INVESTORS?

Because it's glorified as "success" in the eyes of the wantrapreneurs.

Magazines feature and love to write articles about a company that raises money. Egos get big, and the "fake" impression of success is created.

Remember, having investors doesn't equate to success or profitability. It simply means the person was good at pitching their product or solution.

Raising money to grow a legitimate business is not a bad thing. The trouble begins when young, impressionable, would-be entrepreneurs see these lucky recipients of cash injections as Tech Gods and geniuses when all they did was gain investment and obtain an outrageous valuation. This tech folklore is not grounded in reality and gives the wrong impression of what building and sustaining a real business really is.

Often, when entrepreneurs focus obsessively on raising money, they regularly drop the ball when it comes to building a great product or service. The core focus should be on building a viable product that customers are willing to buy.

WHAT IS YOUR BEST EXPERIENCE AS AN ENTREPRENEUR?

My best experience has been the entire process. You have to embrace the process if you are going to be successful as there is no "overnight" success. Becoming an entrepreneur is hard! I've written many articles and responses about how tough it really is, and most people don't realize it.

The good thing is, there are a lot of great things about it. I could talk about many great experiences, but I'll narrow it down to three.

- The satisfaction of building and creating something from nothing and seeing it become successful.
- Creating jobs and seeing the good your company can do. It really makes you realize that we all can have a hand in doing something positive.
- Creating a lifestyle in which I can provide for my family and inspire others the that it can be done.

WHAT WAS THE BIGGEST MISTAKE YOU MADE IN YOUR START-UP?

The biggest mistake I made in my start-up was bringing aboard and hiring the wrong people.

All too often, an entrepreneur can get so excited about their venture that they make quick and fast decisions to move ahead. See, when you are growing fast, you have to fill departments to cover for everything you can't do personally. A startup/ bootstrapped entrepreneur often wears so many hats, and there comes a time, you have to delegate. You just have to make sure you delegate to the right people.

During the startup phase and even during the growth years, a highly energetic person can inspire so many people around them that they attract what we would call, "hangers-on." People who have their own agendas, and those who really don't have the company's best interests at heart. I don't think this is uncommon, but the key is to just be aware of this.

If you bring in these types of people, they may work out for a short time, but gradually, you will see performance drop and morale sink.

Running a business is tough enough as it is, you just have to make sure you constantly have a pulse on your team and never allow the wrong people who aren't 100% "all in" to steer your company off in the wrong direction.

WHAT KIND OF ENTREPRENEUR ARE YOU?

I never even thought of the word entrepreneur as a "career" until I was in my 30s.

When I was in college, I had absolutely no idea what I wanted to do when I graduated. I studied Sociology with an emphasis on Institutional Analysis, but nothing during this time got me excited about business. I watched fellow classmates gain degrees in accounting and business, and I had taken some of these courses as well, but they were dry and boring. The word entrepreneurship wasn't ever mentioned once.

It wasn't until I started working for an insurance carrier a few years later as an adjuster did the entrepreneurial drive kick in. At that time, I still didn't even really identify with the word, "entrepreneur."

It was just a feeling inside that said... I don't want to work here in a cubicle! I have better ideas that can streamline this process of claims, and I want to start my own company servicing a niche I had spotted. I had no real training or knowledge, so I studied up on my own, started reading business magazines, e.g. Inc., Fast Company, etc. and got inspired. Eventually, I took the leap, started small, and drove forward being completely self taught.

Nothing in college prepared me for the challenges of being an entrepreneur, it was my own personal drive and desire teach myself what I had to learn.

Here are a few traits that I do possess, though, that might add to it.

1. I'm very competitive.
2. I hate seeing inefficient processes.
3. I always think about how I can improve on the status quo.
4. I am always coming up with new and creative ideas.
5. I like to lead teams of people.
6. I get excited about great ideas and love to inspire others.
7. I enjoy the challenge of taking on something tough and succeeding
8. I am driven, energetic, and enthusiastic.
9. I have long-term thinking.
10. If I fail at something, I don't give up. I learn from it.

WHAT IS YOUR OWN BUSINESS MANTRA THAT HAS HELPED YOU?

It's a similar version of my mantra when I was playing competitive basketball.

"If you're not working hard and putting in the effort and hours to get better and build the best product or service....., guess what? your competition is. When you meet in the market, they'll beat you." In athletics, it's just a game. In business, it could put you out of business.

I think of business like that every day.

If you aren't consistently doing the things to put your company in the best position to succeed, you won't be successful.

WHAT ARE THE AVERAGE WORKING HOURS OF A CEO?

I have absolutely no idea about any "average" working hours for a CEO.

I can only speak for myself. As a CEO who bootstrapped and built a company from the ground up, there is no such thing as average. You do what you have to when you have to. In a way, you are always on. Now other CEOs may disagree, but I'm speaking from a founder/bootstrapped point of view where you personally put your own skin in the game, and you have everything on the line.

The business becomes a part of you and your lifestyle, meaning it's basically 24/7/365. For me, personally, It's hard to "turn it off." I am constantly thinking about how I can better the company and do the things that can take us to the next level.

See, as the CEO, you are the leader. It all falls back on your shoulders. Sure, you delegate if you hire the right people, but still, the buck stops with you.

You have to have a basic knowledge of all departments and manage effectively. Nothing will ever be perfect or always go as planned, so that's why you have to always have your finger on the pulse. This often requires you to not live a 9–5 mentality.

You work to get the job done, not by hours.

HOW DO ENTREPRENEURS THINK AS COMPARED TO NON-ENTREPRENEURS?

Here's my opinion coming from a person that is often obsessed with creating and innovating.

I think entrepreneurs are obsessed with building something that's better than anything that existed in a particular space and improving on processes. They are usually highly competitive and want to become the best at something. They are thinking up new ideas all of the time, and their minds are working a mile a minute. They are thinking about a new venture to start or how some product or service that could be a "game changer." This thought process occupies much of their time.

Non-entrepreneurs, usually, are not sitting around wondering how they can build a company, create new products, gain market share, and take over an industry. They are more apt to spend their time thinking of other things they might enjoy doing and actually live their life. They have their own interests and goals that are great but simply may not interest an entrepreneur. We all have our own goals and things we are good at. Not everyone wants to be an entrepreneur.

Now let me tell you. Those who are entrepreneurs can be some pretty driven and obsessed people. I know it because I'm driven that way and love it.

While I enjoy it, it might not be the healthiest thing all of the time. The toughest part for me is taking time away and recharging my batteries. I may be wired to forge ahead, but there are many times that I think it's the "non-entrepreneurs" who are actually are more balanced in their life.

There's no right or wrong path that makes entrepreneurs more special than those who don't take that path. Everyone is on their own mission.

WHAT'S THE DIRTY SECRET OF "OVERNIGHT SUCCESS"?

Here's the secret. If you can wait around 10 years, then you'll be the "overnight success" in many people's eyes.

For many businesses, success is merely "little victories" that build daily on top of each other. These victories keeps adding up. The hard work, the grind, hustle, and effort often go unnoticed by most people, including friends and family. People will see you toiling away without really paying attention. In their eyes, you "suddenly" achieved success one day. Why? Because most people aren't paying attention to you. They are focused on themselves.

Then, after slowing building up steam... a decade later, people suddenly seem to notice. "Hey... how did you do it?" "Wait... wow you are that big!"

Eventually, you land larger clients, growth happens, and people suddenly take notice.

The key for any business owner is to focus on building a great company, selling or delivering great products or services, and just keep moving forward. Don't worry about "overnight success." That's for others to discover.

ARE THERE TOO MANY PEOPLE TRYING TO BECOME ENTREPRENEURS RIGHT NOW?

If you have a good idea, there's a market for it, people are willing to pay, and you can become profitable, then there are always opportunities.

Opportunities will always be there, and they always have.

The fact that so many people are jumping in and calling themselves "entrepreneurs" is merely noise.

You can call them business owners, people who want to start a company, etc. etc.

The only reason it seems this way is because so many people are out there "faking" it to appear like they are successful entrepreneurs to create an image. It's trendy, hip, and cool…. or whatever you want to call it.

I didn't think of myself as an entrepreneur ever when I started my company. I just said… hmm, I want to start a company and build a business. I did it, and through a combination of many factors, I've been able to succeed.

I think a lot of younger people get caught up in the hype and pressure in their 20s and feel like they should be the next internet unicorn start-up. They want to live the life without having paid the dues.

Time for some patience.

The field of building businesses will never become too crowded, as in the end, only the ideas that people are willing to pay for will succeed. It's merely market forces. Everything else is just noise.

Don't let the perceived "crowded" landscape of wantrapreneurs discourage you if you have a "true" passion, a great idea, and drive to succeed, but don't even try if you are doing it merely for "status."

Remember, just because someone calls themselves an entrepreneur doesn't mean they are successful. Results are results. If they don't have any, then they are merely fakes.

WHAT ARE THE BEST WAYS TO THINK OF IDEAS FOR A START-UP?

Here's the funny part. I ended up becoming successful in an industry I had NO interest in being in at first. Yes, that's right. I wanted something else but my true path was in front of my eyes.

I tried to co-build an online music/magazine with my brother, I tried to sell real estate, online fitness coaching, helping my wife sell antiques... etc. All with limited success.

I was trying everything I could do to get out of the career I was in, which was insurance. The truth is, I actually knew so much about auto insurance claims that the reason I wanted to leave was because it was an antiquated, paper-centric mess. This was the catalyst that finally got me to start my company! Yes, I was so fed up with seeing the inefficiencies that I said, hell, I will start a company that solves the problem.

And I did.

So what are the best ways to think of start-up ideas? It's to look around right in front of you. Look for the simple problems that can be solved. It might be in a job you are in right now. There might be a vendor that services your company or an area your company has trouble in, and they look outside for help. Look for the niche that maybe someone else has never filled.

Often, it's the niche, smaller solution that can become the most lucrative.

My point is that you don't have to invent the next Facebook, Snapchat, or Uber. You can build a very, very successful business in areas that might seem mundane. Just remember, some niches might already be staring you in the face. You just have to open your eyes.

ARE SUCCESSFUL ENTREPRENEURS GENERALLY GOOD EMPLOYEES?

From my perspective... No.

I had 7 jobs in 8 years, and in my first two, I was fired.

I was a horrible employee. Here's why. I hate mediocrity, and that's what I saw where I worked in every corporate job. During my first few jobs after graduating, I quickly observed how demoralizing the corporate world was. Incompetent and unqualified managers running departments with no drive to increase efficiency or streamline operations. The wheels of innovation never turned. It was stagnant and depressing.

See, the thing is... I didn't realize I was an entrepreneur when I graduated from college. Nobody really used the term much, BUT I had a gut feeling inside that I wanted to start a business. I just didn't know what or how, but I was determined to figure it out.

I have a driven personality and am always coming up with new ideas to improve on processes, new ideas for businesses to start... etc. I began that process during my eight years working the "corporate" lifestyle.

In my free time after work is where I put in the effort. I co-launched an online music business with my brother, I tried online fitness coaching, selling real estate, antiques, and a few other things. All were fledgling attempts to "figure out" this entrepreneur thing.

After eight years working in cubicles, at the age of 33, I was finally ready to take the leap. I studied the competition in my sector and knew I could do better. So, I found a niche in the industry I was in, dove in head first, and haven't looked back.

HOW DO I FIND FUNDS FOR MY BUSINESS IDEA?

First off, if you are looking to start a business that requires a lot of capital to get started and you have no reputation, you won't find any takers.

The reality is that your best bet will be through your own savings, family, or friends at the basic level.

It is very unlikely that anyone outside will invest in someone with just an idea.

Here's the deal, everyone and anyone can have an idea. In fact, almost everyone out there has ideas but they can't execute.

I personally used a combination of my own savings and proceeds my wife and I received from selling our home. We used this money as the initial investment to get the company going. We downsized our lifestyle and took the risk personally. Nobody invested in us nor did I go out and seek money.

Just remember, almost nobody is going to believe in you just because you have an "idea." You have to be fiercely committed to see your dream through and make it happen with the mindset that nobody is going to help you.

The best way to get started after you have fully thought out your business model would be to launch a business that doesn't require much capital. There are a lot of things you can do that don't take much money to get started. I could put out a huge list, but my main point is think of businesses that don't require much investment and go after it!

WHAT IS AN ENTREPRENEUR LIFESTYLE?

It can be different things to different people. With that said, the image of the mansion, Lambo, Ferrari, private jets, and a flamboyant lifestyle may be real for some, but the reality is that is VERY few live like that because much of what you see on the internet is fake.

The internet millionaires and fast cash might lead you to believe that the entrepreneur "lifestyle" is something you are missing out on. It feeds on your dreams and sets unrealistic expectations. In reality, it's not even a lifestyle. That's an "image."

So.... what is an entrepreneur lifestyle?

For a majority of the hardworking businesses out there, it's fulfilling yet super challenging. Remember, though, it's damn hard work!

The lifestyle to me is just that... a lifestyle. That means you basically LIVE your job. There is no 9–5. You don't get to punch out at 5 and detach mentally.

I can't speak for everyone else out there, but to me, I am constantly involved or doing something related to work or thinking about it. As an entrepreneur, the health and success of our company rely on it. The entrepreneur lifestyle for other people may mean different things, but to me, it brings freedom to work when you need to (which is a lot), but you can't take that as a license to just kick back.

Sure, you might be able to take a day off mid-week occasionally and have a flexible schedule, but you'll make up for it working maybe until 1am the next day.

WHAT SMALL BUSINESSES MAKE THE MOST MILLIONAIRES?

I'll keep this answer short.

My experience and observation is that the businesses that do some of the most mundane things are surprisingly the most profitable. It's often the "boring" and non-glamorous businesses that most people ignore that make the millionaires.

Media and hype loves to sell the internet and tech "millions," but in reality, a lot of it is fake hype.

Think of the trades and solopreneur or "small businesses" (plumbing, electrical, HVAC, cleaning companies, freelance consultant firms, private fitness coaches, etc.). The opportunities are out there.

My key point is that many of them may not seem "exciting" businesses to the average person who imagines what a millionaire is like.

ARE SUCCESSFUL START-UPS REALLY ABOUT LUCK?

In a way, there's a bit of luck involved for any business.

The market forces can change at any time, the customer sentiment may vary, and other unseen forces can either make or break a company.

It's not just about start-ups, it's about any business in general. Nothing in business guarantees success forever. Technology is always changing; new products and companies are coming into the market. You just have to be able to adapt as best as you can and make the changes quickly and correctly.

Running a company is like trying to drive down a road that is, literally, changing right in front of your eyes. You can't take your eye off the road.

The best thing a business, start-up, or entrepreneur can do, is to do everything in their own power to put the company in the best position to succeed. You have to set yourself up for success. Even then there is no guarantee you will succeed.

If you work hard, do the best you can, adapt, and with some luck, you can make it happen. So, is luck part of it? Yes, to some degree.

That's my 2 cents.

CAN YOU TELL ME SOME COMMON MISCONCEPTIONS ABOUT ENTREPRENEURSHIP?

Fancy cars
Mansions
Expensive Watches
Laptop on the beach
Work just a few hours a week
Passive income doing little work
Venture capital cash infusions
Internet riches

Those things above are what impress naïve people who think the path toward entrepreneurial success is a status symbol.

We might just be living through one of the times that has the most "fake" entrepreneurs that ever existed. With social media, people can "fake it" and give true aspiring entrepreneurs the wrong impression.

The reality is that entrepreneurship is not those things. Those are some of the trappings one "might" be able to have if they build a highly successful business, but the reality is most successful people aren't that way.

In my opinion, the more talk about lavish vacations, watches, cars... etc., the more likely they are fake.

Just remember, nothing great that is achieved comes easy!

WHEN SHOULD A CEO OF A START-UP STOP "DOING THE WORK" AND LET THE OTHERS DO THE WORK?

In my experience, the CEO should stay focused and engaged until the time that he or she has a competent leadership team in each core department.

The catch, though, is that it is different for every company. There's no magical number of staff or employees you have to reach. It's about competent and reliable leadership in each spot.

Having come from a "bootstrap" mentality, I remain actively engaged in managing and running the company I built for over 15 years.

I did make the mistake of stepping back in a few areas and entrusted the wrong people in certain departments and paid the price for it. The company morale in those areas, as well as productivity, plummeted. I had to step back in and regain control.

The key is finding amazing people who have your vision and who are loyal to you and the vision of putting the company first in all decisions. When you have people in departments trying to hide information and create leverage by making themselves indispensable, they have to go. You need team players not those looking out for themselves.

Roughly, I would say if you have 50 employees or less, you have to remain engaged on a day to day level. Once you start to grow beyond that, you will have to rely on leaders to assist.

Your major focus as a start-up should be to remain very engaged in all areas and ONLY relinquish oversight once the leaders you bring in demonstrate excellence. Then your goal is to hold them accountable for success in their respective positions.

WHAT IS THE BEST WAY TO ENTER A SATURATED MARKET?

Generally speaking, it's not a great idea to enter a saturated market. You spend most of your time in price battles, and it's a race to the bottom. Avoid it if at all possible.

If you do decide to jump in, it's best to find a niche within the market and go after it hard. The niche is where you can carve out a great business.

Going head to head in a crowded market is tough because you have to differentiate yourself and really stand out among all of the noise.

In a saturated market, you need to focus on delivering a technology, service, or solution that is superior than anything in the market, provide exceptional customer service and stand out from the rest. You're marketing has to separate you from all of competitors. Any effort you think is good enough is likely to keep you in the crowd, so you have to think 10X. You have to do 10 times as much as anyone else to get noticed.

Go after the niche, grab market share, and expand.

IS SOME DEGREE OF IRRATIONAL OPTIMISM NECESSARY TO FOUND A START-UP?

You bet!

You have to have a mindset that believes to your core that what you are building is such a game changer that nothing can stop you. You have to believe that you are better than any competitor, and your company WILL succeed. It must succeed.

You have to bend reality, because if you live by the "status quo" where most people reside, you'd never succeed. Simply being average and thinking just the "normal" way doesn't lead to big success.

You have to live it, breathe it, and believe in yourself and in what you are doing.

You'll have to ignore the haters, the doubters, and those who think you are almost crazy. In life, most people let that small stuff hold them back from their dreams. That's why you have to embrace the drive and "irrational" belief that you can make it happen.

Nothing guarantees success, but if you do all the right things to put yourself in a position to win and succeed, then you have given yourself the best odds.

Why wouldn't you want to tip the odds in your favor?

Focus on driving forward with positive action, and give it your all.

HOW CAN I CONTINUALLY KEEP MYSELF MOTIVATED?

Here's the deal... We all go through our own ups and downs in life. You can't be motivated 100% of the time. Life happens. That's okay, it doesn't mean you are a failure, loser, or are weaker than others. Too often, we might even think everyone else around us is powering forward while we are stuck. It's not true. Like I said, we all have ups and downs.

Here's my formula for staying motivated.

1. **I stay active.** I ramp up my activity and output. For example, if I feel slightly down and things aren't going the way I want, I dial up my positive activity and action. See, the key is recognizing that if you are "lacking" motivation, you were obviously motivated about something to begin with. Hit the reset button and up your action!

2. **Seek the small wins.** Too often, when you have big goals, anything less doesn't seem satisfying. The reality is that small victories can re-ignite your passion and fire from within. Focus on the little things that add up. Each successive "win" and accomplishment builds on the next, creating fuel for your engine. Before you know it, all of this positive activity has you back on track!

3. **Eliminate negativity.** Sometimes our motivation will drop because we allow negativity to slowly creep into our lives and not even realize it. It could be friends who make sarcastic comments or family that express doubt. These little negative seeds can sprout and destroy your drive. Cut out the negativity, and you likely will see your motivation return.

4. **Don't discount health factors.** Sometimes you'll feel your motivation has dropped, but you're being too hard

on yourself. A hard driving person who wants to achieve could see motivation sink due to simply suffering an injury, getting sick, suffering emotional stress, poor diet, and lack of sleep. If all of these factors aren't dialed in, you could easily feel as though your motivation has dropped.

WHY IS ENTREPRENEURSHIP CONSIDERED A LONELY JOURNEY?

It's a lonely journey because it's the route most people would rather not take. There are no guarantees of success, and it's a hard road. The average person wants more simplicity in their life. Less risk and less stress.

It's easier to get up, drive to work, sit in a cubicle, get a paycheck, party with friends, have 2 days off for the weekend, and start all over again.

See, that's the easy way. The path of least resistance.

For entrepreneurs, though, unless you have supportive family members and friends, is a solitary road. While you are toiling away on your vision, other people are out living life, having fun, and moving on.

In a way, you can feel alone and isolated.

It's hard for others to really identify with you. They don't know what you are going through and pay very little attention.

I remember going to "extended family" events, and relatives were out swimming, having fun, and barbecuing while I was locked away in my office handling urgent matters to keep my company going. They wondered why I only came out to eat and had to head back in.

Ten years later, they have seen the success I created and were shocked. For them it seemed like "overnight success."

They didn't see me toiling on the lonely road for a decade.

In reality, though, most businesses fail, and for an entrepreneur, you are taking a risky path with little guarantee for success. You have a mission, you are likely driven and passionate. You have to go it alone, or at least, with few believers on your team.

But you know what, it's the pioneering spirit, desire to take the different path, and inner fire inside that others don't have that can lead to success. While it may be lonely on the journey, if you can make it work, it is well worth the effort.

Just remember, entrepreneurship isn't for everyone, and that's okay.

For those who go after it, go after it full steam, and give it your all!

HOW CAN I MOTIVATE MYSELF TO WORK HARD?

First off, everyone is motivated to do something, even if it's simply to sit on the couch and watch TV or play video games.

The trick, though, is how do you motivate yourself to achieve things that are tougher. Things that require HARD WORK.

Well, let's be honest. Nobody can be motivated 100% of the time. We all have limited energy. Even the most dynamic and driven people all have the same 24 hours a day and go through various levels of energy and drive.

So.... how can you motivate yourself to work hard? Don't try to simply motivate yourself. In fact, much of motivation is a myth. There's even a book out there called "The Motivation Myth" by Jeff Haden. It's a good read!

Motivation in the sense of the traditional "motivation" by getting pumped up and fired up is merely a form of a sugar rush. It's like eating ice cream and candy. It tastes good, you enjoy it, and the sugar rushes through your body. Then.... Boom, you crash.

That kind of motivation won't last through the tough times. For that, you need discipline, routine, and a focus on small victories. All fueled by consistent and unrelenting action.

Here's how I believe you get it done.

1. **You dial up your outputs and activity.** When you stop sitting around and take action and produce more activity, that in itself gets the engine going. Whenever you feel your "motivation" is low. Get moving, do things, get in motion, and increase your output.

2. **Create routine.** Working hard and achieving goals require a consistent and daily routine. Whatever it is you want to accomplish, you have to do something every day that supports your progress toward the goal. It must be something that's not negotiable, and you do it day in and day out. There's not instant overnight success here, it's daily consistency.

3. **Keep a log or journal.** Write it down. I keep a daily workout journal and notes of my daily activity. It reinforces your routine and documents it. Why? Because you can see how far you come, take notes on what worked and what didn't. It also allows you to go back sometime in the future and rediscover what was working when you were on your path. It also lets you see all of the obstacles you overcame. Document your journey.

4. **Focus on the "small" victories.** Success and ultimate achievement is merely a compilation of thousands of tiny little wins you gained along the way. It's the growth, the experience, the knowledge, and work that instills the fire within me. The victory is IN the journey. This IS the motivation, because once you achieve the goal, you know you had the "motivation" to make it happen.

5. **Don't underestimate the power of your health.** Many of us feel "unmotivated" not because we are lazy or unable to achieve and work hard. We are simply not fueling our bodies properly or you aren't getting enough sleep. Change your diet into eating super healthy, get rid of the alcohol, get proper sleep, and you will feel energized like never before.

So, if you want to be motivated to work hard, you need to realize that there is no magical "motivation" tool that will suddenly give you instant, long-lasting motivation. It has to come from within by doing things like I mentioned. Little victories create motivation, and then the cycle repeats over and over through consistency. That's how you achieve.

WHAT DO YOU DO WHEN YOUR SALES BUCKET IS EMPTY OF NEW LEADS?

From my perspective, when you need to ramp up sales, you first and foremost need to have an active pipeline. If your pipeline of leads is empty, that's a big problem.

If your pipeline is empty, you need to quickly start thinking about...

What can you do to load it up?

1. You have to get active and take action. It can be stressful when the pipeline is empty, but what can you do to generate more leads? Start to brainstorm.
2. Revisit deals that you almost had but the leads didn't close. Is there a chance you can re-pitch to them and win?
3. Get active in social media. Engage potential leads there
4. Ramp up thought leadership in your industry. Write articles and publish those that show your expertise.
5. If your business is online, conduct webinars. If you are local, network.
6. Check in with every cold lead you had and revisit them.

The key is to 10X your activity when you're needing to build the pipeline. Massive social media, write articles, reach out to old contacts, and go to where the prospects in your industry are. Bring the energy and enthusiasm to it, and the prospects will see it.

SOME PEOPLE SAY NOT TO WORRY ABOUT COMPETITORS WHEN STARTING A BUSINESS. WHY IS THIS?

I think a lot of people say that as advice meaning.... "Don't spend all of your time worrying what others are doing when you need to be focusing on what you can do to make your product or service the best that it can be."

With that said, you must know your industry inside and out, though, and stay vigilant to what is transpiring in the marketplace, otherwise, you could get blindsided by something you didn't expect.

Build the best product or service, differentiate yourself from the competition, and keep innovating and improving your service and solutions.

Business is hyper competitive, and if you aren't pushing ahead, building momentum, marketing, selling, and bringing the energy and enthusiasm, your company won't succeed.

Focus on being the best company you can, and have a product or service you fiercely believe in so much that any customer would want to choose you over anyone else. Remember, in any market, those who get positive attention and are top of mind with the customer, often win.

AS A FIRST-TIME START-UP ENTREPRENEUR. HOW DO I MOTIVATE MY PARTNERS?

First off, if your partners are not motivated, that's a bad sign.

Building a company is one of the toughest challenges out there. The odds are stacked against you in the first place. Most businesses fail, and from day one, you have to be driving forward full steam ahead just to get yourself in a position to succeed. All you can ever do is put in all of the hard work as much as possible to set yourself and your company up for success. There are no guarantees, so with that in mind, you have to have a highly motivated team all united toward one goal. The difference between success and failure can be razor thin.

If your team is not 100% on board, I'd hit this topic head on with them, because you won't succeed with unmotivated people.

Better to address it now instead of letting it go on.

HOW "PERFECT" DOES A START-UP FOUNDER HAVE TO BE?

Nobody can be perfect ,and there's no "ideal" when it comes how "perfect" you have to be as a start-up founder.

Everyone who has amazing skills in one area is likely horrible is some other area.

We often see the "perfection" of people who are the business icons because media and society focuses on their genius but rarely their shortcomings.

So how perfect do you have to be?

You have to be the best YOU that you can be in the areas you are good at. Then you surround yourself with the best people you can find in the areas you are weak in.

You might be great at vision, creativity, and inspiring a huge team, but could be miserable at managing day to day employees.

Don't feel bad. You don' have to be great at everything. You should have a general working knowledge of all areas and have a desire to learn and grow but nobody can master everything.

That's why you build a "team" of experts and skilled people to support your vision.

So there is no amount of "perfect" you need to be. What you need to be is authentic and be yourself.

WHAT ARE CONS OF BEING A LEADER?

1. The buck stops with you. You have to take responsibility for leading a team, and the results fall back on you. Good or Bad. You have to be able to handle that stress and elevate your entire team's performance.
2. You have to be able to handle large amounts of stress, which can come from different angles. Customers, employee

issues, service or product issues, and be able to juggle various tasks.

3. You have to be comfortable being the "lead singer." You are the focal point for good and bad. You are going to be the face of your team or company so you have to enjoy that to some degree or at least be comfortable with that.

4. You can't control everything. Business is hard, and success is never guaranteed. Things can go great for a period of time and quickly change not due to any fault of your own. All you can do is set your company and team up for success by doing everything in your power to tip the odds in your favor. You can't put all of the pressure on yourself because you simply can't control everything.

WHEN, IF EVER, DOES IT MAKE SENSE FOR A COMPANY TO HAVE CO-CEOS?

No. Never.

Every company needs a leader at the top. This person is the visionary, the person who inspires and drives the company mission. The title means nothing, though, because it's how you lead and what you do that counts.

The only time such an arrangement is usually proposed in smaller companies is when another founder feels they want the ego title to make themselves feel good.

A company isn't run to give people titles to impress their friends and fulfill personal goals. A company first and foremost is in business to make money and succeed.

What you can have is a great backup team, though, that is built of solid top-quality executives who excel in each area and can essentially run the company smoothly without the CEO having to step in all of the time.

As for co-CEOs. Nope.

DOES HARD WORK GUARANTEE SUCCESS?

Here's the deal....

NO. Hard work doesn't guarantee anything. You could put in the effort, do everything right, and still fail.

Unfortunately, that's life.

The reason so many people focus on hard work as a key to success, **and rightfully so**, is that many people don't want to put in the effort. Those who do, dramatically increase their odds of success.

So if hard work doesn't guarantee anything, what can you do?

You can set yourself up for success. That means if you do the work and everything goes right, you have greater odds of winning.

Here's how you do it?

You put in the effort, do the work, plan the best that you can, do everything that can tip the balance in your favor, and then simply give it your best! That's all you can guarantee.

When it's all said and done, you know you gave it your all.

I WANT TO BECOME AN ENTREPRENEUR ONE DAY, SHOULD I MAJOR IN FINANCE OR ACCOUNTING?

No major or degree is needed to become an entrepreneur. Sure, either can "help" and assist you in running a company, but becoming a business owner or entrepreneur is more than what degree you choose. If you really want to learn, start doing and start learning on your own. Read books on entrepreneurship, study successful people, and start a side business.

Becoming an entrepreneur comes from within. It's a drive to build something, create a product or service, see it through, and make it happen.

A driven entrepreneur is more about being a creator, leader, innovator, and visionary. All of the academic elements are great, but over time, you can easily hire amazing people in each of those areas to assist you. You should gain a good overall knowledge in the finance and accounting areas, but eventually you have to hire pros.

My advice would be to major in what you are truly interested if you go that route, but just realize the "degree" doesn't mean you'll be a successful entrepreneur.

You would be far better served by actually jumping in and starting a small business and start learning in real life. This is where you gain the real experience and know how that's needed. My best experience was working in a start-up with my brother while I worked my day job and also tried various other business ventures.

IS IT A GOOD IDEA TO START A START-UP STRAIGHT OUT OF COLLEGE?

You can start a company anytime. It's never too late, but here are my thoughts...

Why not start a side business now or work as an intern at a company while you are in school? This way, you are building some "real world" skills. Be a sponge and soak up as much knowledge as you can.

Anything you can learn while you are in school and to start getting your feet wet in business is all going to help.

I took a safe path, got a job out of college and was stuck on a paycheck, I quickly realized I hated it but it was hard to get out. I started several side businesses but most failed. This, in hindsight, was my learning phase. All of this Kept pushing me forward to become an entrepreneur. Had I done some of this in college, I would have been much farther down my path.

Finally, I took the leap full-time after seven years in the corporate world and built my company. Now looking back, I wish I did it sooner.

Don't wait to go after your dreams. Life's short, so go make it happen.

WHAT IS MORE VALUABLE: SUCCESS OR FAILURE?

Success, while great at the moment, is often fleeting. It's never permanent as someone else or some other company is always out there looking to beat you, and you know what... you can never win all of the time.

Success can, at times, be partly due to luck or circumstances that people misinterpret for skill, and this can lead to an overconfidence that is unwarranted. They then don't know how to handle failure and can't seem to recover. Don't let that be you.

So while success is great, you have to also understand that failure is always on the horizon, and you'll meet it at some time. Through failure, you have to recalibrate and not see it as "failure" but really as feedback. This is where some of your biggest growth can happen.

Each (Success and Failure) provide an opportunity to grow, better yourself, and move toward what you should be looking for... happiness.

WHAT ARE THREE DAILY HABITS THAT HELP YOUR SUCCESS?

1. **Exercise every day.** You don't have to blast your body every day with intensity, but you need to do something. I keep it simple. I walk 45 minutes through the hills. Bike 20 minutes at varying speeds on a mountain bike, and Lift weights/or resistance training

2. **Meditate.** I personally use the Muse headband. I've been able to train my brain to get in a calmer state much faster. You don't need the headband, but at least take time out to simply be in a calm environment and just relax. I used to not believe in it, but I do now. It leads to a much more focused and calm outlook.

3. **Stay hydrated.** It sounds simple, but many times we don't realize that we are dehydrated. It can be from the foods we eat or simply the dry air. Lack of proper hydration gives me a headache or I can simply feel a bit tired or off. You don't need to go overboard but just make sure you drink enough water. For me, it can make a huge difference.

As you noticed, all of these were about your health and mental outlook. If you aren't taking care of your health and mind, you can't be optimized to perform your best and feel great. These daily habits help set me up for success.

WHAT ARE SOME UNCOMMON WAYS TO WORK SMARTER INSTEAD OF HARDER?

In a world where we often feel we have to do more and more and more, we can adopt a more stoic mindset.

To paraphrase Roman Emperor Marcus Aurelius:

In every case one should ask themselves: " Is this, or is it not, something necessary?" And the removal of the unnecessary should apply not only to actions but to thoughts also.

If you operate that way, you'll be focusing on what's important, thus working smarter, and at the same time, you'll be much less stressed.

WHAT WAS THE VERY FIRST ACTION YOU TOOK TO START YOUR CURRENT START-UP?

I took out a notepad and wrote down my basic ideas and drew some rough diagrams. That was the start.

WHAT DO START-UP FOUNDERS TYPICALLY GET WRONG WHEN STARTING A BUSINESS?

There are a ton of things that a founder can get wrong, but in my opinion, here are three you need to think about.

1. **Not truly having a product or service that people really want.** Too many people today think that they can quickly come up with a trendy idea or app, and suddenly, they have a business. Remember, just because you can create an app to do something doesn't mean it has value.

2. **Partner with the wrong people.** In the "exciting" moments of starting a company and launching, everyone is so pumped up to get the company going they often fail to really ask themselves... "Can I seriously work with this person, and are they really committed to the company for the long-term?"

3. **Expecting quick adoption of your product or service.** Reality check... we live in a society where there is constant noise of new start-ups, apps, social media... etc. Obscurity is one of the biggest things a business has to overcome. Nobody knows, or likely cares, you have an app or business. You have to put in the work to get noticed. A lot more than you think.

HOW IS IT POSSIBLE FOR A NON-TECH BACKGROUND CEO RUN A TECH STARTUP?

How is it possible? Very simple.

True leaders can rally, inspire, direct, and drive success almost anywhere.

Remember, all successful companies and ideas don't come from developers and those with a tech background. There's an illusion or myth in some circles that the leader or CEO needs to have a heavy tech foundation, and I think much of that is based on the "coder/founder" idea that we see with some of the unicorn companies that get a lot of press. There's a lot more to being a CEO than having a tech background.

The reality is that a CEO in a tech startup needs some working knowledge of technology and how the development process works but the vision and leadership can come from a non-tech person. In fact, a business is much more than coding and technology. You have to have organization, marketing, sales, finance, and structure. Just having a nice piece of technology means absolutely nothing if you can't sell it.

The technology team is there to execute on the vision. They are to build what the company leaders ask and make it great. Just because someone has a great technology background doesn't mean they are the least bit qualified to lead.

The determination whether a company succeeds or not often depends on all of the other factors working in conjunction with technology to make a company a winner.

HOW CAN A CEO DELEGATE WITHOUT PEOPLE THINKING HE OR SHE ISN'T WORKING?

A CEO must delegate. If you don't, you'll end up doing everything.

Here's my perspective as an entrepreneur and CEO of a company I built from the ground up.

Starting out, I did pretty much everything. As I grew the company, I had to delegate to people in different departments. The key, though, is delegating to those you can trust to get the job done.

As far as worrying what people think. You simply don't worry about it. It's that simple. What they don't know, and often, will never understand is that the CEO has to "run" the company, and that is far more than being siloed into one specific department or job. The ultimate responsibility lies with you, and just because people think you have it easy doesn't mean you have to even entertain their thoughts. Just do your job, be authentic, and build a great company.

Never worry about trying to impress or show others that you are doing something just for the sake of creating an impression. Results matter. Worrying what others think is a waste of valuable time.

HOW MANY HOURS DID YOU PUT INTO GROWING YOUR BUSINESS BEFORE IT BECAME SUCCESSFUL?

Countless hours that I never counted.

Here's the thing, though. If you are driven and passionate about what you are doing, you don't even think about it.

There's no magical number of hours you have to put in. You put in what you have to put in.

You work and keep working at it until it works.

Also, keep in mind, there is no guarantee of success. You can put an immense amount of hours in and still fail.

You have to really believe in what you are doing and the product, service, or solution you are selling. You keep at it until you make it happen.

A version of "success" gradually happens. You make some sales, you grow a bit. You have some ups and downs and maybe grow some more.

That's why goals are great but you need to break things down into smaller pieces, and when you string a group of small wins together, you finally start to see it all come together.

Hours? Who knows.

BE EXTRAORDINARY!

I want to inspire you to greatness, and I hope this book fires you up to go out and achieve your dreams! I want to leave you with an article I wrote that I think encapsulates what's most important.

THE VICTORY IS IN THE JOURNEY.

You ever wonder why when you achieve a goal you feel a little empty inside?

It's okay to admit it.

It might not hit you right away, but eventually, the basking in your glory, the accolades, and encouragement from your friends and family fades, and the trophy, award, or medal begins to collect dust.

Merely an object or reminder to what you have done in the past.

Sounds depressing?

Sure, it might be.

Why is achievement fleeting?

Why does the figurative climb to the top of the mountain leave you lacking that eternal sense of accomplishment?

Because life is about moments. It's about NOW.

The past fades, and the future is in front of us, and who wants to live in the past?

Hey, when I was younger, all I could think about was driving and forging ahead and knocking out goal after goal. Half-Ironman races, marathons, job promotions, finishing classes, winning awards, and building a sense of "internal" fame. I felt that I couldn't let up, had to keep pushing and checking off more and more things on my "list."

All to keep achieving goals to be successful, or what I deem successful and gain more recognition.

Now, there's nothing wrong with being driven to achieve! In fact, you should always be striving to become better, grow your skills, knowledge, and your definition of "success."

In life, you should test yourself, push yourself, and leave the uncomfortable to get uncomfortable. That's how you grow.

What I was ignoring, however, was every little step along the way. Sure, I'm a huge believer that massive goals are achieved by small, little victories that add up over time, and when put together, equal ultimate achievement.

Sure, that's great.... BUT, I wasn't truly living those "tiny" victories. I was doing them in mind and body but not truly relishing the moment of each one.

I wasn't focusing on enjoying the journey. I was pushing from one success to another, seeing it as merely a quick step on the run toward my mythical endpoint of perceived success. Like something just out of reach, there is inevitably one more thing to do. One more hill to climb.

Before you know it, you've passed a huge chasm but don't know how you really got there. Much like taking a walk through nature, but because you are on the phone the entire time, you don't notice anything you walked by. You never see the flowers, the trees, or wildlife. It's like driving home on mental autopilot and not knowing how you got home because you are operating like a robot. You never noticed life along the way.

We live in a world today so interconnected, so digitally consumed, that we are under a constant barrage of tweets, likes, updates, news, shares, and alerts, that we can rarely decompress. We never really take the time to reflect and enjoy the moment.

We never enjoy the journey.
The journey, though, is life!
This is where we live, grow, and shape who we are.

So my point is this. While we should drive ahead, achieve, and push for improvement, goals, and success, don't forget to actually live and truly **enjoy the journey,** because that is where most of us live our lives.

Go out and live your dreams!

—Ernie

ABOUT THE AUTHOR

ERNIE BRAY drives success. He's a 6 time Inc. 5000 CEO, entrepreneur, author, speaker and business coach who built an award-winning national business. Fed up with the corporate world, Ernie took the entrepreneurial leap and bootstrapped a company from the ground up with no outside investment into one of the fastest growing private companies in America.

He now runs a leading technology firm in addition to being a regular contributing writer for Forbes, Entrepreneur, HuffPost, TechCo, business.com and various other outlets.

Drawing upon his fifteen years building a successful company, he is also a business coach helping aspiring entrepreneurs, startups and businesses through erniebray.com and one-on-one personal coaching. His passion is helping inspire others to get out and drive their own success!

www.ingramcontent.com/pod-product-compliance
Lightning Source LLC
Chambersburg PA
CBHW021928190326
41519CB00009B/949